NEGATIVE THEOLOGY

NEGATIVE THEOLOGY

A Short Introduction

Johannes Aakjær Steenbuch

CASCADE *Books* · Eugene, Oregon

NEGATIVE THEOLOGY
A Short Introduction

Copyright © 2022 Johannes Aakjær Steenbuch. All rights reserved. Except
for brief quotations in critical publications or reviews, no part of this book
may be reproduced in any manner without prior written permission from
the publisher. Write: Permissions, Wipf and Stock Publishers, 199 W. 8th
Ave., Suite 3, Eugene, OR 97401.

Cascade Books
An imprint of Wipf and Stock Publishers
199 W. 8th Ave., Suite 3
Eugene, OR 97401

www.wipfandstock.com

PAPERBACK ISBN: 978-1-6667-4216-9
HARDCOVER ISBN: 978-1-6667-4217-6
EBOOK ISBN: 978-1-6667-4218-3

Cataloguing-in-Publication data:

Names: Steenbuch, Johannes Askjær [author].

Title: Negative theology : a short introduction / Johannes Aakjær Steenbuch.

Description: Eugene, OR: Wipf & Stcok Publishers, 2022 | Includes bibliograph-
ical references.

Identifiers: ISBN 978-1-6667-4216-9 (paperback) | ISBN 978-1-6667-4217-6
(hardcover) | ISBN 978-1-6667-4218-3 (ebook)

Subjects: LCSH: Negative theology | Negative theology—Christianity | Negativ-
ity (Philosophy) | Christianity—Philosophy | Mysticism | Spirituality

Classification: BT83.585 S74 2022 (print) | BT83.585 (ebook)

VERSION NUMBER 091922

Cover illustration: Jean-Léon Gérôme, *Moses on Mount Sinai* (1895–1900)

Whoever searches the whole of Revelation will find therein no doctrine of the Divine nature, nor indeed of anything else that has a substantial existence, so that we pass our lives in ignorance of much, being ignorant first of all of ourselves, as human beings, and then of all things besides. For who is there who has arrived at a comprehension of his own soul?

—GREGORY OF NYSSA (C. 335–95 AD)

Contents

Preface

How do we speak about what cannot be said? How do we speak about God if God is ineffable? These paradoxical questions lie at the heart of one of the strangest traditions of philosophical and theological thought: negative theology. As a tradition of thought, negative theology goes back to the convergence of Greek philosophy with Jewish and Christian theology in the first century. Beginning with a seemingly simple claim about the ineffability or unsayability of God, negative theology evolved into a complex tradition of thought and spirituality. Today, together with a growing interest in patristic and medieval studies, negative theology enjoys renewed attention in contemporary philosophy and theology. While much has been said and written about negative theology in recent years, my impression is that there is still a need for a short introduction to a theme that can sometimes seem impenetrable by its very nature.

It may be argued that the main insights, problems, and enigmas of negative theology are far from being exclusive to this particular tradition of Western philosophy and theology. Other religious and philosophical traditions have been equally aware that the deepest truths about the universe and human existence cannot be put into words. During the Middle Ages, Islamic and Jewish philosophers developed their own versions of negative theology. It could also be argued that it bears certain similarities to Eastern philosophy and religion. However, it would be a step too far to investigate these similarities, even if there may have been influences from, for example, Indian philosophy in late antique Neoplatonism.[1] This short introduction does not attempt to provide a comprehensive overview of negative theology in all its complexities, but only to tell a generally coherent story about what has been said about what cannot be said.

As such, this short introduction is confined to describing the tradition as it evolved from late antique Greek, Jewish, and Christian thinking through the Middle Ages and into contemporary philosophy and theology. This should be more than enough to begin with, which is also why much has been left out for the sake of brevity and narrative coherence. The purpose is not to say everything there is to say about negative theology, but only to give a brief overview of the tradition. Those who are interested in a more thorough investigation may gain some impression of where to dive in, though I will not throw in too many references. Instead, I provide a list of suggestions for further reading at the end of the book. Many of the texts discussed in the following pages are available in William Franke's two volumes of *On What Cannot be Said* (University of Notre Dame Press, 2007) on which I rely heavily. I have also made good use of Deirdre Carabine's *The Unknown God* (Peeters Press, 1995) as well as Denys Turner's *The Darkness of God* (Cambridge University Press, 1995) and Raoul Mortley's *From Word to Silence* (Hanstein, 1986), even if I do not always agree with their conclusions.

I have used the most easily available translations of texts quoted, while also providing my own translations when needed (this is also the case for Bible quotations). When referring to ancient texts I use the commonly used English titles in the footnotes. Some of the material is based on my Ph.D. dissertation from 2014 about the relationship between negative theology and ethics in early Christian thought. The practical consequences of negative theology are also dealt with in this introduction. I hope to make it clear that we are not just dealing with some obscure activity of

---

1. See Knepper et al., *Ineffability: An Exercise in Comparative Philosophy of Religion* and Franke, *Apophatic Paths from Europe to China*.

speculative thought, but with a living engagement with the mysteries of faith and philosophy—one with real-life implications.

Thanks to Benjamin Marco Dalton, William Franke, George Karamanolis, Søren Gosvig Olesen, and Kristoffer Garne for comments on the manuscript.

—Johannes Aakjær Steenbuch

Nylars, Denmark 2022

INTRODUCTION

What Is Negative Theology?

"NO ONE HAS EVER *seen* God, but if we love one another, God lives in us and his love is made complete in us" (1 John 4:12). These words from the First Epistle of John—and other similar statements made by New Testament authors—capture a core element of what was later to be termed "negative theology." Simply put, negative theology is a form of theology that talks about the divine by using negations: God is *in*effable, *in*visible, *un*limited, *in*finite, *in*comprehensible, and so on. For modern readers, unfamiliar with theological reasoning, the term "negative theology" may sound like an objection to theology, or even like atheism or nihilism. The original purpose of talking about God in Christian theology in this way was, however, neither to deny the existence of God, nor to promote the kind of agnostic indifference to religious matters that is widespread in contemporary post-modern societies. Its main purpose was to emphasize that faith exceeds mere objective, theoretical knowledge. Faith is, as in the case of the First Epistle of John, a matter of *practice* rather than just theory. We cannot know God through abstract concepts, but by faith and love we live in and participate in the reality of God.

Nevertheless, there is also a more obviously "negative" side to negative theology. Early Christian apologists often applied negative definitions of God in their attacks on pagan religion. If God cannot be known, seen, and comprehended, then everything we worship as idols must be rejected. Only later did negative theology become what can be called a speculative practice. At this point, pagan, Jewish, and Christian philosophers alike developed negative theology as a way of speaking about the otherwise ineffable God. In particular, this took place in the highly eclectic philosophical and religious milieus of first- to third-century Alexandria, Egypt. Beginning especially with the Jewish philosopher Philo of Alexandria (c. 15 BC–50 AD), negative theology evolved in the Christian philosophy of Clement of Alexandria (150–215) and the pagan Neoplatonism of Plotinus (205–70). From that point on, negative theology developed in parallel in both Neoplatonism and Christian philosophy. This development culminated in the sixth century with Dionysius, whose synthesis of the Neoplatonism of Proclus Lycius (412–85) with Christian and Jewish doctrine became definitive for theology in the Middle Ages, not least as expressed by John Scotus Eriugena (815–77), Moses Maimonides (1138–1204), Meister Eckhart (c. 1260–c. 1328), and Nicholas of Cusa (1401–64).

Often, negative theology is also called apophatic theology, from the Greek word *apophasis*, which can mean "denial" or "negation." As such, *apophasis* is typically understood in distinction to *kataphasis*, or talking in positive, affirmative propositions. Strictly speaking, though, *apo-phasis* means "un-saying." When used as a rhetorical device, *apophasis* is a means of bringing up a subject by denying it ("I will not mention that . . ."). When applied to theology, this kind of negation can be understood as a kind of theology that "unsays," withdraws, or retracts our concepts about the God we can perhaps have faith in, but not comprehend. God is *not* finite, God is *not* visible, God is *not* comprehensible, God can *not* be put into words, and so on. This is negative theology or *apophasis* in its most basic form. More broadly defined, however, negative theology can be thought of as any kind of discourse that emphasizes God's ineffability, infinity, incomprehensibility, invisibility, and so on, even if such negative definitions are not used explicitly.

It may perhaps be argued that negative theology, for this reason, can by its very nature not be defined precisely. It is not as obvious as may seem at first sight that two instances of negative theology are actually parts of the same discourse, since the very object of negative theology cannot be defined in positive definitions. By its nature the meaning of negative theology is highly context-dependent as apophatic definitions always depend on what they deny. Negative theology cannot, for this reason, be abstracted from its wider theological, philosophical, religious, or even polemical, social, and political context. This should be kept in mind when considering negative theology as a tradition or history of thought.

Negative theology, despite its name, has rarely been applied for purely negative purposes. As already suggested, while applying negations to our definitions of God, negative theology does not for this reason deny the core beliefs of, for example, Christian theology, such as the divinity of the second person of the Trinity incarnate as Jesus Christ. On the contrary, negative theologians in the Christian tradition usually affirmed that God has revealed himself fully in Christ. But by doing so, God becomes *both fully hidden and fully revealed*, as Maximus the Confessor (580–662) would explain with reference to the Chalcedonian creed, where Christ is said to be both fully divine and fully human. Negative definitions of God are needed to *preserve the mystery*, as some Eastern Orthodox theologians are prone to say. The purpose is to avoid confusing our theology and dogmas about God with God himself.

The rejection of traditional metaphysics in the late Middle Ages led to new perspectives on negative theology. Following the Reformation in the sixteenth century, large parts of medieval philosophy and theology were rejected by Protestants and replaced by what was claimed to be a more scriptural approach to theology. Negative theology did not disappear, however, but took on novel forms as a result of the new emphasis on human depravity and the need for grace. With the speculations of Jacob Böhme (1575–1624) in the seventeenth century and strands of German idealism in the nineteenth century, once again, negative theology became influential in philosophy and theology. The somewhat "mystical" approach of medieval negative theologies was, nevertheless, often rejected by modern theology. In the twentieth century, Protestant theologians such as Karl Barth, Lesslie Newbigin, and Eberhard Jüngel criticized traditional forms of negative theology for being too influenced by philosophical speculation, or "the spirit of Plato."[1] They argued that we should focus on God's revelation in Christ, since the idea of "the hidden" or "the unknown" God could easily become an excuse for inventing a God determined by us.[2] The true God is, however, revealed in Christ independently or even in opposition to whatever ideas and definitions—negative and positive alike—we may have of God.

Those adhering to some form of negative theology have typically replied that the opposite is just as much or even more the case: negative theology is, again, necessary so that we do not confuse our images and ideas of God with God himself. This, perhaps, explains why today negative theology enjoys renewed interest, especially among those who seek a vision of faith beyond the simplistic alternatives of fundamentalism and atheism. Negative theology points to a third way between or beyond two extremes that both fail to address the mystery at the heart of theology. I will not go into too much detail about these discussions, however, but only attempt to outline the wider historical narrative that informs some of the contemporary interest in negative theology.

The first part of this book deals with the development of negative theology in late antique philosophy and early Christian theology. It focuses on how negative theology played an important role in the development of Christian orthodoxy. The second part deals with how negative theology evolved in the Middle Ages, focusing on the Neoplatonic idea of God as "beyond being." This notion of God resulted in some rather radical forms of mystical theology that would help to shape how we conceive not just God and the world but also human identity and freedom. The third part deals with how negative theology was reshaped before, during, and after

1. Jüngel, *God as the Mystery of the World*, 223.

2. "The unknown god is a convenient object of belief," said Newbigin critically, "since its character is a matter for me to decide." Newbigin, *The Gospel in a Pluralist Society*, 21.

the Reformation, and how new kinds of negative theology have appeared in recent years. Today, theologians take a growing interest in negative theology, as do philosophers with a more secular perspective. This has arguably resulted in what could be called the secularization of negative theology, leading to what is sometimes perceived as forms of negativism and nihilism. In conclusion, I will briefly discuss how the alleged nihilism of postmodern philosophy has been criticized by so-called Radical Orthodoxy, while also pointing to some suggestions as to how engaging with classical forms of negative theology may take us beyond the nihilism often associated with secularized negative theology.

I

The Beginnings of Negative Theology

The people remained at a distance, while Moses approached
the thick darkness where God was.

—EXODUS 20:21

WHILE JESUS AND HIS disciples roamed the Palestinian territories,
just a few hundred kilometers west of Jerusalem the great city of
Alexandria had become a melting pot of religious and philosophical schools, sects, and ideas. Here, a peculiar encounter would take
place between Greek philosophy and the biblical narratives. The
Jewish philosopher Philo of Alexandria, a contemporary of Jesus,
and the first Christian apologetic theologians in the generations
after him, struggled to formulate their faith in philosophical terms.
This project required the development of new ways of thinking
about the fundamental principles of reality. Philo emphasized the
ineffability of God, while early Christian apologists, in defense
of Christianity, applied negative theology as a means of asserting
the distinction, peculiar to the biblical worldview, between God

and creation. While the purpose was often polemical, Christian theology arrived at a still more advanced understanding of what it means to talk about the ineffable God, thanks to the likes of Clement of Alexandria. Meanwhile, perhaps in conversation with Christian thinking, Neoplatonic philosophers like Plotinus developed their own version of negative theology, one that continued to be at the center of disputes about what was to be considered Christian orthodoxy in the following centuries. The culmination in the Christian context was the highly sophisticated negative theology of the Cappadocian theologians in the fourth century. With Gregory of Nyssa we arrive at what may be considered that classic formulation of negative theology in the early patristic period. As we will see, this negative theology was not only a matter of theory, but also had important implications for the perceptions of spirituality, anthropology, human freedom, and ethics.

The Judaic-Hellenic Roots of Negative Theology: The Bible, Philo of Alexandria, and the Middle Platonists

Although negative theology became a staple of philosophical theology during the Middle Ages, to a large extent, the roots of negative theology are pre-philosophical. In the Hebrew Scriptures, the strangeness and hiddenness of God is a recurrent theme. Consider, for example, the story of Job, who cannot accept the sufferings that befall him: While his friends try to make sense of Job's sufferings by reasoning about God's justice, the young Elihu declares that "The Almighty is beyond our reach" (Job 37:23). When God finally appears to Job and his friends, it becomes obvious that human beings are incapable of reasoning about God, making the vanity of their arguments clear. In the famous discourse on the vanity of the world, Ecclesiastes makes a similar point, exhorting: "God is in heaven and you are on earth, so let your words be few" (Eccl 5:2). Other passages in the Hebrew Scriptures describe God as a God who hides himself (Isa 45:15) and even as having made darkness his hiding place (Ps 18).[1]

This strange concept of God hiding in darkness is a core element of what was to became the favorite narrative in negative theologies: The story of how God first revealed himself to Moses in a burning bush (Exod 3:4), and how Moses was later to meet God in a dark cloud (or "thick darkness") on a mountain (Exod 20:21), while finally being denied a direct vision of God's face (Exod 33:20).

Negative theologies found a deep spiritual meaning in this story. Origen of Alexandria, in his polemics against the pagan philosopher Celsus, argued that Moses was the first who really understood that the highest good, God, cannot be put into words.[2] This was not something that Moses learned on his own by philosophical reasoning. Rather, he had to experience it by meeting God as God revealed himself to Moses. In this way, Moses was believed to have become the founder of a spiritual tradition, that would eventually inspire even pagan philosophy.[3]

Although there were precursors, as a philosophical discipline negative theology has its beginnings in the great first-century Jewish philosopher Philo of Alexandria. Philo, who has been called "the father of negative theology," understood the story of Moses as a narrative about God's ineffability. While Plato had acknowledged that it is indeed "hard to find out" about the creator and father of the universe and even harder, if not impossible, to communicate this knowledge to all, Philo is arguably the first to describe God as "ineffable" or "unsayable" (arrētos in Greek).[4] As put by the traditional Greek translation of the Hebrew Scriptures, the Septuagint, God had described himself to Moses simply as ho ōn, "The One who is" (Exod 3:14).[5] Philo took this as expressing that no more

---

1. Ps 17 LXX (Septuagint).

2. Origen, *Contra Celsum* 6.4.

3. According to many early Christian apologists, Plato had stolen or copied his doctrines from Moses.

4. Plato, *Timaeus* 28c.

5. In modern translations, which focus on the Hebrew 'ehyeh 'asher 'ehyeh,

can be said of God, since God, who is "being itself" (*to on*), is as such beyond human understanding and language. Philo says that when Moses approached the "thick darkness" (or, depending on one's translation, the "dark cloud") where God was, while the people stood at a distance, this refers to God's "incorporeal and invisible essence" that cannot be comprehended by any human being.[6] What Moses realizes is that we have no power in us that can comprehend "the living God." This was also why it was that when Moses on the mountain wanted to see God's face, he was only allowed to see God's back: "you cannot see my face, for no one may see me and live" (Exod 33:20). God, in other words, reveals himself only *indirectly* to Moses. Philo took this to express the idea that the *existence* of God may be known through his works in creation, but the *essence* of God, God *in himself*, is beyond our understanding.[7] This was not, however, all that there was to say. Having met God on the mountain, according to the story in Exodus, rays of light were shining out from Moses's face (Exod 34:35). As would be noted by later commentators, this should remind us that although God dwells in darkness, God is not darkness *per se*, but a kind of "luminous darkness" as Gregory of Nyssa would formulate it. God is incomprehensible light, and the person who experiences God will likewise become radiant, as Moses did to such a degree that he had to carry a veil over his face.

Philo of Alexandria believed he had discovered deep philosophical truths in the narrative about Moses. Perhaps drawing on the Neopythagorean philosophy that gained some popularity a century before, Philo could describe God as existing in unity.[8] In Pythagoreanism the Monad was understood as a mathematical principle beyond all beings, perhaps identical with the idea of

---

it is "I am who I am" (Exod 3:14).

6. Philo, *On the Change of Names* 7–14. In other works, Philo applies a distinction between God's incomprehensible essence (*ousia*) and God's comprehensible activities (*energeia*) that was to become central to later negative theologies. Philo, *On the Special Laws* 1.47–49.

7. Philo, *On the Posterity and Exile of Cain* 166–69.

8. Philo, *Who Is the Heir of Divine Things?* 183.

the good in Plato's *Republic*.[9] Philo, who was later referred to by Clement of Alexandria as "the Pythagorean," likewise emphasized God's unity and simplicity of being. God is beyond all the peculiar properties that characterize created things. God's being is simple, not in the sense that it is easy to understand, but in the sense of not being composed of more basic stuff.[10] God has no parts. This also means, however, that from divine simplicity follows God's ineffability, since what is absolutely simple cannot have any other nameable characteristic.

Another fundamental principle in the negative theology developed by Philo was that things can only be named by something higher.[11] Since God is the first principle, God cannot be named or comprehended by anything created. God is unlike any human being or the sun or the moon or the stars, says Philo. God is only like himself, though even this description is imprecise as it makes God an object of human language.[12] God can be described through his works, as the creator, but as the first principle of everything, God is ineffable.

This notion of God's ineffability might have been taken up by other Alexandrian philosophers after Philo. In the second century, the philosopher Alcinous, often described as a "Middle Platonist," likewise explained in his famous *Handbook to Platonism* how God is ineffable and cannot be known as he is. Since God does not possess any attributes, he is neither bad, nor good, nor the same as anything, nor different from anything, since nothing distinguishes him from other things.[13] Nevertheless, says Alcinous, we can gain some notion of God through the ways of abstraction, analogy, and eminence. While the latter two may be considered positive ways, the way of abstraction is the more negative. It proceeds, Alcinous

9. See Carabine, *The Unknown God*, 46–48.

10. Philo, *On the Unchangeableness of God* 55.

11. Raoul Mortley has even described this idea as the "Philonic principle." See Mortley, *From Word to Silence*, 133.

12. Philo, *Questions and Answers on Genesis* 2.54.

13. Alcinous, *Handbook of Platonism* 10.4–6. Thanks to George Karamanolis for reminding me of this important reference.

explains, by abstracting all attributes from God, much like how we can form the conception of a point (i.e., a mathematical object with no dimensions) by abstracting dimensions from physical objects. As a mathematical method this was not new, but it seems to have been original as applied to theology.

Whether Alcinous and other Platonists of the second century were inspired by Philo is a matter of ongoing discussion by scholars.[14] If Philo was actually the source for the notion of God's ineffability in later Platonism, then Origen may not have been completely off in his claims about the Judaic origins of the by then widespread notion that God cannot be put into words. But while the extent of Philo's influence on pagan philosophy in Alexandria is debatable, his influence on early Christian apologetic is more apparent.

Known and Unknown: The First Christians

With the first Christians, the world was to witness new and radical claims about God. God was no longer hidden in darkness, but had revealed himself in a human being, Jesus Christ: "The one who looks at me is seeing the one who sent me," Jesus had said to his disciples according to the Gospel of John (John 12:45). Still, although revealed, God remains invisible: "No one has seen God," says John in his first epistle, although "the only begotten Son has made him known" (John 1:18). Similarly, the First Epistle to Timothy—perhaps alluding to Elihu's words in the Book of Job—describes God as one who "lives in an unapproachable light, whom no one has seen or can see" (1 Tim 6:16). Later, negative theologies were to describe this "unapproachable light" as paradoxically identical to the darkness that God had made his hiding place, according to Psalm 17. The point seems to be that God is only known through revelation and that even if revealed, God is still in some sense incomprehensible.

14. Wolfson, "Albinus and Plotinus on Divine Attributes," 115. The theory that Philo influenced Neoplatonism in this has, however, been contested by later scholars. Carabine, *The Unknown God*, 75, 94.

As we have seen, the First Epistle of John emphasizes the invisibility of God, but an important addition is that God is known in love: "No one has ever seen God, but if we love one another, God lives in us and his love is made complete in us" (1 John 4:12). This could be taken to mean that a comprehensive theoretical conception of God is not possible, but that God is known in practice as love. A similar point is made by Paul when he argues that "knowledge puffs up while love builds up." Those who think they know something, says Paul, "do not yet know as they ought to know." However, much like John, Paul adds that "whoever loves God is known by God" (1 Cor 8:1–3). Faith is not so much about *knowing* but rather about *being known*. On a different occasion, Paul explains that, being new creatures in Christ, "we regard no one from a worldly point of view" (or "according to the flesh") (2 Cor 5:16). This too reflects the First Epistle of John, which similarly emphasizes that it is not yet revealed what the "children of God" will be (1 John 3:2). The new creation in Christ is a gift of an unfathomable grace that cannot be grasped by the human mind, which is why faith is needed to perceive it.[15]

In other words, for the authors of the New Testament, there seems to be a close connection between negative theology and the new existential and ethical realities that follow from the belief that Christians have been adopted by God through Christ. As argued by some contemporary theologians, this also has to do with the Christian understanding of God as love. If "God is love" (1 John 4:8), then God cannot be this or that "thing" since love is only something to the degree that it gives itself to others.[16] Christ's love "surpasses knowledge" (Eph 3:19) just as the peace of God "transcends all understanding" (Phil 4:7), which are arguably positive ways of saying that these things are more or less incomprehensible. Love cannot be made an object of thought because it only exists in relations. We shall see later how negative theology also had significant implications for views on human freedom and dignity, but

15. This was the recurrent theme of Karl Barth's classic commentary to Paul's Epistle to the Romans. Barth, *Romans*, 149–87.

16. Marion, *God without Being*, 47–48.

for now, it suffices to notice that the biblical claims about God's hiddenness and invisibility rarely, if ever, serve a purely speculative purpose. The point is primarily ethical, having to do with how God relates to the world and how people relate to God in practice.

This, however, is not all there is to say about the sources of negative theology in the biblical scriptures. When Paul made his famous speech on the Areopagus in Athens, he made reference to "the unknown God," who was worshiped by some of the Athenians: "You are ignorant of the very thing you worship," says Paul, "even if God is not far from any of us." In fact, God is the one in whom "we live and move and have our being," as Paul puts it, using a quotation from the Cretan philosopher Epimenides (Acts 17:23–28). In this way, as later theologians would often see it, a somewhat philosophical idea of God as "the unknown God" in whom we nevertheless participate, becomes the negative starting point, the empty space, so to speak, that must be filled by the positive proclamation of the good news about God's revelation in Jesus Christ.

For the early Christians, philosophy became instrumental in formulating theological doctrine.[17] Developing a negative theology as a point of connection was arguably a way for early Christian thinkers to combine philosophy with the gospel message without confusing the two. In this project, Philo's negative theology proved useful for the early Christians. Philo's distinction between *God*, who is ineffable, and *the works of God*, which can be known, reappears in early Christian apologetics. Justin Martyr (c. 100–165), who is famous for his early synthesis of Platonic philosophy with Christian theology, argued that God, being the father of all, is "ineffable." He added that even "God" is only a notion that we apply to something we can hardly explain: "To the father of all who is unbegotten there is no name given," says Justin, arguing that "by whatever name he be called, he has as his elder

17. Many early Christians, like Justin Martyr and Clement of Alexandria, did not see Christianity as distinct from philosophy altogether, but rather as the perfect philosophy. See Karamanolis, *The Philosophy of Early Christianity*, 24–54.

the person who gives him the name."[18] In this way Justin affirms Philo's belief that since God is the source of all being, God cannot essentially be put into words by human beings, who, being created, are on a lower level than God. We do have the ability to talk about God, but words like "Father," "Creator," "Lord," and even "God," are not really names, says Justin, but "appellations derived from his good deeds and functions." Justin points out, perhaps somewhat surprisingly, that even the name "Christ" contains an "unknown significance," though the name Jesus, his name "as a human being," has significance in relation to his works of salvation. Again, negative theology is applied to remind us that our words for God are not abstract definitions but refer to concrete relations.

The idea that God, as uncreated and radically distinct from creation, is ineffable and indescribable can be found in a good number of subsequent Christian apologetic theologians around the Mediterranean. Like Justin, Aristides of Athens (d. c. 134) argued that God, who is uncreated and without beginning, does not have a name, as anything that has a name must be associated with the created order.[19] Whatever seemingly positive name we use to describe God must be understood as an implicit denial, saying what God is not. For instance, when I describe God as "perfect," says Aristides, this simply means that there is no defect in him—a negative claim. In the same vein, Theophilus of Antioch (d. c. 185) explained that God is ineffable and indescribable, but God can be known through his works: "For if I say He is Light, I name but His own work" and "if I call Him Wisdom, I speak of His offspring."[20]

Somewhat original to Theophilus was the belief that God created the world "out of nothing" (or *ex nihilo* as the subsequent tradition calls it). While Tatian (c. 120–80) together with the Shepherd of Hermas, an anonymous writing from the second century, had already suggested that God "made all things out of nothing," it was Theophilus who developed this idea in more detail. He did so against Platonic philosophers who held that matter was unbegotten

18. Justin Martyr, *Apology* 2.6.

19. Aristides, *Apology* 1.

20. Theophilus, *To Autolycus* 1.3.

and was thus, in *some* sense, divine. However, Theophilus insisted that *only God* is unbegotten, which is what makes him ineffable and indescribable to created beings who are not divine. Matter is thus not eternal. Consequently, the material cosmos must have been created "out of nothing." In this way negative theology affirms the "Christian distinction" between God and everything else.[21] In Carthage, Tertullian (c. 155–240) also held that God is beyond all our conceptions. The "immense" is known only to itself, as he puts it in his *Apology for the Christians*. Tertullian argued that our very inability to fully grasp God is exactly what affords us an idea of God. In this way, God is presented to our minds as "at once known and unknown."[22]

As already argued, for early Christians, this was much more than just a theoretical point. The ineffability and incomprehensibility of God was crucial in early Christian polemical engagement with pagan culture and religion. Simply put, if God as the creator is beyond comprehension, then nothing worshiped as God in creation can be identical to the true God. For example, Justin Martyr, in one of his apologies, complained that pagan idols, being made of corruptible material, are insulting to God who has "ineffable glory" but has his name associated with things that are corruptible.[23] In the same vein, the unknown author of *The Epistle to Diognetus* polemicized against the pagan worship of statues, but also against Jewish religion, arguing that if God is invisible and in need of nothing, there can be no need for ritualized religion, fasting, and offerings. Likewise, Tatian argued that the ineffable and invisible God should not be presented with gifts, being in need of nothing.[24] Theophilus similarly argued that since God created all things out of nothing, only God is in need of nothing. In this line of thought, God did not *have* to create the cosmos but rather *freely chose* to create all things out of nothing in an act of pure gift.

---

21. Sokolowski, *The God of Faith and Reason*, 32.
22. Tertullian, *Apology for the Christians* 17.
23. Justin Martyr, *Apology* 1.9.
24. Tatian, *Address to the Greeks* 4.2.

A Dream of the Truth: Clement of Alexandria

Turning back to Alexandria in Egypt, the great Christian philosopher Clement of Alexandria (c. 150–215) also makes the claim that God, the creator of everything, is "in need of nothing." Clement, who is famous not least for his eclectic approach to philosophy, is often considered the first Christian theologian to systematically make use of negative theology.[25] Although critical of pagan culture, Clement shared with Justin Martyr a somewhat positive evaluation of Greek philosophy and poetry compared to many other early Christian apologists. Justin had argued that philosophers before Christ also took part in the divine Logos, the Word of God that had become human in Christ as described in first chapter of the Gospel according to John. Similarly, in a passage in his *Exhortation to the Greeks,* Clement poetically describes Greek philosophy as having a "dream of the truth." However, the wisdom of the Greeks seems to have been mostly negative in kind, as when the "truth-loving" Plato declared that it is impossible to communicate God to everyone, and the comic poets ridiculed pagan religion.[26] In this way, pagan philosophy and even poetry can play the role of a "schoolmaster" similar to that of the Law and the Prophets in the Hebrew Scriptures by pointing to Christ allegorically. According to Clement, God was known by the Greeks in a gentile way, by the Jews judaically, and by the Christians in a new and spiritual way.[27]

Clement's greatest achievement as a writer is arguably his *Stromateis* or *Miscellanies,* a collection of books that deal with a variety of philosophical and theological topics in a deliberately unsystematic way. In these books Clement affirmed Philo's allegorical reading of the narrative about Moses who entered the "thick darkness" on Mount Sinai, although he does not go as far as Philo did when the latter argued that the "darkness" refers to God's essence. The darkness is only preliminary to God's revelation. God, being above space and time, is not, says Clement "in darkness or

25. Hägg, *Clement of Alexandria,* 3.
26. Clement, *Exhortation to the Greeks* 6.67.2.
27. Clement, *Stromata* 6.5.41. Cf. Gal 3:24–26.

in place."[28] For Clement, the "thick darkness" primarily refers to the ignorance of the mob, which Moses had to leave behind in order to know God, who is invisible and ineffable.[29] The darkness of ignorance is dispelled when we acknowledge our ignorance and start seeking the truth in faith.[30] This is because God can only be known as he reveals himself through faith. As the first principle of everything, God is ineffable and incomprehensible, but God can be known as revealed through his Word, the Logos.

Clement affirms the distinction between God and everything else as expressed by the doctrine of creation out of nothing. Having created everything from nothing, God has "no natural relation" to creation.[31] For Clement, this meant that God only reveals himself indirectly. Even in the incarnation, God has revealed himself as veiled in a human body. Clement affirmed the Christian belief in the divinity of Jesus Christ, but he made it clear that God hides himself in his revelation. This seems to be exactly why faith is required to perceive that Jesus was not just another human being.[32] Again, negative theology reminds us of the necessity of faith.

Clement, however, also had to consider the possible abuse of negative theology in his encounters with its more radical forms. These radical forms appeared in the Gnosticism that competed with the strains of Christian theology that were later to be considered orthodox. A generation before Clement, theologians like Basilides and Valentinus had developed theological systems where God was not just described as ineffable but also as "not even ineffable." According to Hippolytus of Rome, Basilides had claimed that God did not even exist in the beginning, but that before anything existed, there was altogether "nothing." As absolutely "nothing" this "nothing" cannot be named, not even by describing it as "ineffable."[33] In making this claim, Basilides may have been

28. Clement, *Stromata* 2.6.1.

29. Clement, *Stromata* 5.78.3. Cf. Philo, *On the Special Laws* 1.47–49.

30. Clement, *Stromata* 5.17.3.

31. Clement, *Stromata* 2.74.1.

32. Clement, *Stromata* 5.34.1.

33. Hippolytus, *Refutation of All Heresies* 7.20.

polemicizing against Philo's Judaic philosophy, a suggestion made plausible by Basilides's apparent claim that God himself originated in "nothing" before being.[34] At any rate, such claims are clearly at odds with the understanding of God *as "being"* based on God's description of himself to Moses as "The One Who *Is*" in the Septuagint translation of Exodus 3:14. For gnostic theologians like Basilides, the creator God, the "demiurge," while perhaps residing at the top of the hierarchy of being, is still lesser than the true God, which is not a part of this hierarchy at all. It may be true that the God of the Jews created the world, but since the world is evil, the God that is referred to in the Hebrew Scriptures as "The One Who Is" cannot be considered the highest God. For Basilides, the true God cannot even have being, and for this reason cannot be named *at all*, not even by being called ineffable.

Other gnostic sources, like the later *Tripartite Tractate*, based upon the teaching of the theologian Valentinus, also emphasized the inscrutability and incomprehensibility of the true God. An important difference in comparison with the Jewish negative philosophy of both Philo of Alexandria and of later Christian theologians is that for the gnostics it was not only God's *nature* that was unknowable, but *also his existence*. For the gnostics, creation may say something about the *creator God*, but it does not reveal *the true God* that resides on a higher level.

Defending the goodness of the biblical God and his creation was a primary concern of orthodox Christians like Clement of Alexandria, who rejected the claims of the gnostics like Basilides and Valentinus. Clement could sometimes talk about the virtuous Christian using the term "gnostic" (meaning "one who knows"), but unlike in Gnosticism, he did not consider the gnostic to belong to a completely different category from the ordinary faithful Christians. In order to defend the goodness of God and his creation, Clement went on to develop his own orthodox version of negative theology rather than simply discarding it altogether. Where Gnosticism claimed to have a certain knowledge ("gnosis") of divine things, Clement insisted that God, as the first principle,

---

34. Carabine, *The Unknown God*, 85.

can only be the object of faith. As nothing is more fundamental than God, God can only be related to in faith. Clement argued in this way that all knowledge presupposes faith. As formulated later by Anselm, we believe so that we can understand.

God is not just the first principle but is also to be understood by his unity and simplicity. The father of the universe has no parts, Clement explains in an important passage in the fifth book of his *Stromateis*.[35] As such God can be identified as "the One" (*to hen*). The One is per definition indivisible, says Clement, but as such it is also infinite (*apeiron*). That the One is infinite means that it has no dimensions or limits, which is also why God does not have any form or name. Since the One is without form and name, this means that not even "the One" or "Being" or "God" are proper names for God. Names for God are no more than points of support that help to direct our thoughts about God while still not comprehending God as such.[36] This line of reasoning is important since what we have here is one of the earliest identifications of God as "infinite." Clement may have been drawing on Plato's dialogue *Parmenides*, as Plotinus a generation after him would do much more systematically (more on that below), but Plato had not described God as infinite. In Greek philosophy infinity had often been considered to be more or less synonymous with imperfection, but for Clement it becomes a way of safeguarding the ineffability of God.

The only way to reach a conception of God is by going through a process of "contemplative analysis" where we gradually remove all dimensions and properties from physical objects.[37] Through this process of abstraction we will eventually arrive at a point, or unity. In this Clement may have been drawing on the philosopher Alcinous, as described above. Clement adds, however, that we must eventually leave even this point behind. We do this by casting ourselves into "the greatness of Christ," which is where Clement obviously departs from pagan philosophy. By doing so we will arrive at a holiness that consists in knowing God, but "not what he is,

35. Clement, *Stromata* 5.81.3–4.
36. Clement, *Stromata* 5.82.1.
37. Clement, *Stromata* 5.71.4.

but what he is not," says Clement. This is when God reveals himself through "his own power," the Logos that is revealed through the incarnation and the cross of Christ.[38] Negative theology can, in other words, only lead us to silence. We only become truly capable of listening to God as we stop talking and let God speak instead.

This does not mean that we cannot, then, speak about God at all, but it does mean that our language can only *indirectly* point at God. That God is beyond human language is why, for Clement, truth can only be communicated through metaphors and allegorical language. Since God cannot be directly expressed in speech, words can only point indirectly to God. This also explains why Clement wrote his books in a deliberately unsystematic manner. Of course, this was also why Jesus spoke in parables. That truth cannot be captured in writing does not, however, mean that the written word is of no value. Clement had a high view of Scripture. The voice of the Lord, who is himself the Word of God, speaks through Scripture.[39] We must, however, move beyond the bare letters in order to perceive the spiritual truth in Scripture. By using negative theology or "dialectics" as a tool, it is possible to break open the hard shell of language that contains the kernel of truth, so to speak.

This approach, informed by negative theology, made it possible to read the Hebrew Scriptures allegorically, and in this way defend the Christian belief in the goodness of the creator God against Gnosticism, even if at times the biblical narratives apparently speaks of things unworthy of God. However, at the end of the day, truth as such can only be approached through silence. For Clement, this becomes an important element in his understanding of prayer as a kind of silence, which unites us with God's Spirit through "boundless love," as he puts it.[40] To relate to God in full

38. Clement adds that when Moses asks God to show himself, the point is that God can only be known by his own power as revealed through our co-crucifixion with Christ on the cross: "it was not without the wood of the tree that He came to our knowledge. For our life was hung on it, in order that we might believe." Clement, *Stromata* 5.71.5.

39. Clement, *Stromata* 7.95.4–5.

40. Clement, *Stromata* 7.44.6.

intimacy, we must eventually get rid of language. As such, negative theology arrives at a point of highly spiritual significance, making it much more than just speculative philosophy or a polemical tool.

The One Beyond Being: Plotinus and Neoplatonism

While developments in the Christian approach to negative theology were largely connected to the discussions on the nature of God as incarnated in Jesus, a somewhat different kind of negative theology evolved alongside Christian theology from the second century on. Alcinous explained how the ineffable God can be approached through a process of abstraction. As described in the above, a similar approach appears in Clement, although he added that God's ineffability follows from the fact that God is the One and as such infinite and unnameable. Numenius, another Middle Platonic or Neopythagorean philosopher of the second century, similarly argued that there is a first God who is unknowable, although identical with the good, which he also described as the One.[41]

It was, however, the philosopher Plotinus (240–70), who, in the generation after, recognized the full consequences of the notion of "the One" as identical with the source of all being. Plotinus, according to his pupil Porphyry, had studied philosophy in Alexandria under Ammonius Saccas, whose other pupils may have included Origen and other Christians. Whether Ammonius was himself a Christian was a disputed issue among Christians and Neoplatonists in late antiquity, but at any rate it seems that there must have been a convergence of Platonic and Christian philosophies in Ammonius's school. Porphyry also relates how the teachings of Ammonius inspired Plotinus to investigate Persian and Indian philosophy. Although critical, Plotinus may also have been partly influenced by gnostic theologians in Alexandria.[42]

First of all, however, Plotinus based large parts of his philosophy on Plato's dialogue *Parmenides*. In this dialogue, the eleatic

41. Numenius, *Fragments* 19.
42. Porphyry, *Life of Plotinus* 16.

philosopher Parmenides had presented a head-spinning argument concerning "the One" (*to hen*). If the One is really one, then it can have no parts, but since a beginning and an end constitute parts, the One must be without beginning and end, and therefore, it must be infinite and eternal in the sense of being timeless. The One cannot even have being as this would also constitute a part. Also, the One cannot be seen as identical to or different from anything, as also Alcinous had said in his characteristic of God. Of course, we should not be surprised if this makes knowledge about the One impossible.

Curiously, while Plato saw the arguments about the One as exercises above all in intellectual "gymnastics" and as "play-things" (so described by Plato himself), later Platonists, at least from Plotinus onwards, quite consistently made the One the foundational element of their philosophy. In Plato's dialogue *The Republic*, Socrates had once described the good as "beyond being" (*epekeina tēs ousias*).[43] This enabled Plotinus to identify the One with the good. In the good, everything that exists has its origin, even though the One itself is beyond being. This re-appropriation of Plato's idea of the One has been described as "one of the oddest turns in the history of thought."[44] Now the One is not, as with Plato, simply paradoxical and impossible, but the source from which all being emanates. The One is simple (*haplous*), unmixed and pure, but it is nevertheless the cause of all multiplicity in the world. Since the One is simple it cannot have thought, since thought is always made up of a duality by the thinking subject and the object that is thought about. Plotinus, for this reason, rejected Aristotle's definition of God as the unmoved mover *that thinks itself*.

The One is *beyond being and thinking*. As such it can only be contemplated through a negative approach. Since the One is above all duality, in order to be united to the One, the human soul must leave behind all multiplicity and duality. What Plotinus at one point describes as the "flight of the alone to the alone" partly

---

43. Plato, *Republic* 509b.

44. Guthrie, *A History of Greek Philosophy*, Vol. 5, 33–34. See also Franke, *On What Cannot Be Said*, Vol. 1, 11.

resides in a negative theology that "removes" or "abstracts" every notion about the One or the good. Our thought cannot grasp the One, says Plotinus, as long as any other image remains active in the soul. Only by putting everything that pertains to the intellect behind us through removal, can we become one with the ineffable One that is beyond all discursive knowledge and duality. "Remove everything!" (*afele panta*) is the battle cry of Plotinus's negative theology.[45] Only by removing or abstracting *all* attributes from the One can we reach a conception of the One.

In this Plotinus typically talks about abstraction (*aphairesis*), similar to the Middle Platonists and Clement, rather than negation (*apophasis*) in the strict sense. Plotinus, however, like Clement, emphasizes that it is not enough to reach a notion of unity in order to think of the One, but that we must eventually leave this notion behind too. It is unclear whether Plotinus was drawing on Christian authors such as Clement in this, but Plotinus's philosophy obviously shares certain traits with the negative theology developed by contemporary Christian thinkers—even though Plotinus goes further in his claims that the source of all being, the One, is beyond all being itself. Plotinus also drew ethical conclusions, and, like Clement, he believed that in order to commune with the One, the human soul would have to ascend and rise above the plurality of the world. The aim is to become one, an event or a process sometimes described as *henosis* in which the human soul rids itself of everything foreign to it. The soul must be set free from all outward things, Plotinus explains, and turn wholly within itself, with no more leaning to what lies outside. You must, he says, "forget even yourself, and so come within sight of that One."[46]

Plotinus's rather intellectual approach should not diminish the fact that, for the Neoplatonists, just as for their Christian contemporaries, philosophy and theology had a wider practical and ethical purpose. Philosophy was a way of life, as the French historian of philosophy Pierre Hadot famously put it, but this also means that negative theology had implications beyond the mere

45. E.g., Plotinus, *Ennead* 5.1.8; 5.3.17; 6.9.4.

46. Plotinus, *Ennead* 6.9.7.

theoretical realm. Nevertheless, analogous to theological abstraction and negation was often an attitude of distance to political and social life, from which it was thought the philosopher should free himself. This is not to say that Plotinus's philosophy was completely apolitical, but only that it resulted in a somewhat detached attitude to politics and social life. If possible, however, the person who has come close to the One should teach others about how such communion can be achieved.[47]

As hinted at above, scholars have often discussed the likenesses and differences between Christian and Neoplatonic negative theologies. Some argue that while there are similarities at face value, the aim of Neoplatonic negative theology was to remove the differences between levels of reality in order to make the continuous more clear.[48] In distinction, the purpose of negative theology in the Christian context was more often to stress the fundamental difference between God and everything else. It would take us too far to go into this discussion here, although it should again remind us that negative theology was not a monolithic thing based on one specific worldview. It is equally true, however, that most if not all negative theology in the Middle Ages, whether Christian or not, would to some degree be influenced by Plotinus and Neoplatonism.

As Neoplatonism developed into a tradition of its own with Plotinus's pupil Porphyry, it continued to compete with Christianity for centuries, at least as far as intellectuals were concerned. Later Neoplatonists like the Syrian philosopher Iamblichus (245–325) would combine Plotinus's though with theurgic practices as a more ritualized way of relating to the Divine that is beyond intellectual comprehension. Iamblichus—like also Damascius (458–538), the last proper Neoplatonist some centuries later—added to Plotinus's philosophy the idea that beyond the One there must be an even more ineffable principle. Such radicalism may itself seem a plausible reason why Christians were skeptical about Neoplatonism. However, Christian authors often borrowed from

47. Plotinus, *Ennead* 6.9.7.
48. Mortley, *From Word to Silence*, 539.

the Neoplatonists. While, at times, this led to fierce discussions and allegations of heresy, the negative theology often associated with Neoplatonism could also be wielded in defense of orthodoxy. It thus came to play an important role in the theological disputes of the third and fourth centuries, as we shall see in the following examination.

On the Verge of Orthodoxy: Arianism, Marius Victorinus, and the Cappadocians

Negative theology continued to play a more or less prominent part in the theological discussions in Alexandria. For Origen, who lived in Alexandria at the same time as Plotinus, negative theology played a somewhat subordinate role as a description of how human beings lack an understanding of God as long as they are without the Spirit. While affirming that God is to some degree ineffable, Origen rejected the Platonist philosopher Celsus's claim that God was beyond being and as such completely incomprehensible.[49]

There were other similarities between parts of Christian and Neoplatonic thinking. The Father, Son, and Spirit in Christian theology were sometimes understood in parallel to the three levels of reality in Neoplatonism, the One, the Intellect, and the World Soul. At times, the Christian alignment with Neoplatonism even led to a theoretical subordination of the Son, making him secondary to God the Father. Hence, new controversies related to negative theology arose in the fourth century when the Alexandrian priest Arius (c. 256–336) became the center of controversy due to his claims that Christ was not God but a created being. Apparently, Arius had made the argument that God, being the "monad," is also completely "other" (*allotrios*) to everything. As such God is ineffable and incomprehensible even to the Son, who is essentially "alien" to the Father.[50] While Arius was defending strict monothe-

49. Origen, *Against Celsus* 7.45. See also Carabine, *The Unknown God*, 63.

50. Athanasius, *Letter Concerning the Decrees of the Council of Nicaea* 6.1.4–5; *On the Synods* 15.3.9; *Against the Arians* 1.6. See also Stępień and Kochańczyk-Bonińska, *Unknown God*, 62–66.

ism, it is not surprising that his claims were seen as denigrating the status of Christ. To counter Arius, orthodox theologians like Athanasius of Alexandria (d. c. 373), firmly insisted that the Father and the Son share a common essence. While the Father may be essentially incomprehensible to human beings, the Son knows the Father, as was also attested by the canonical Gospels (e.g., Matt 11:27). This view of the Trinity was to become the basis of orthodox theology as expressed by the Nicene creed of 325.

The example of Arianism may seem to suggest that it was an excess of negative theology that led to heretical views. Negative theology in its radical, Neoplatonic version could also, however, be used against Arianism. This is clear from the example of Marius Victorinus, a Roman rhetorician and Neoplatonic philosopher, who had converted to Christianity in old age. While Christian philosophers had usually followed Philo in defining God as "The One Who Is," based on God's description of himself to Moses in the Septuagint translation of Exodus 3:14, Victorinus followed Neoplatonic philosophy in seeing God as *"beyond* being." There was a polemical point against Arianism in this. Arians argued that like the world, God's Son, the Logos, was created "out of nothing," and could not, for this reason, be divine. Against this view, Victorinus argued that while it is true that the Logos comes from nothing, this nothing is *the divine* nothing, which is, however, only nothing in the sense of being beyond being. God is, says Victorinus, in this sense "no-thing" (*me ōn*) as he is not among the things that have existence.[51] This is why God is unknowable, but the Son and the Father, although two, are One in divinity.

Arianism did not disappear, but its arguments changed. This became apparent when the Neo-Arian theologian Eunomius of Cyzicus (d. c. 393) argued that God the Father and the Son must be essentially different from each other, as the one is said to be essentially "un-generate" (or "unbegotten") while the other is essentially "generate." Eunomius argued that these names express the essences of the Father and the Son respectively, so they cannot have the same essence. While Arius seems to have held a radically

51. Marius Victorinus, *To Candidus* 13.5–12.

negative theology in his original dismissal of trinitarian orthodoxy, Eunomius seems to have taken the opposite stance in claiming to know a perfectly precise description of God's essence. Because of the rationalistic nature of Eunomius's claims, when orthodox theologians sought to defend trinitarian orthodoxy against Neo-Arianism, a moderate form of negative theology became useful again. This is especially clear in the theology of the Cappadocian theologians: Macrina the Younger (324–79), Gregory of Nyssa (335–95), Basil of Caesarea (330–79), and Gregory of Nazianzus (329–90).

In one of his theological orations against Neo-Arianism, Gregory of Nazianzus explained that thinking about God is like riding wild horses. As soon as we think we understand something, we lose our grip and learn that we are farther away from the truth than we ever would have imagined. Although we know that God *exists*, the conviction of a thing's existence is quite different from knowledge of *what it is*.[52] We know that God exists, but we cannot grasp God's ineffable nature with our limited minds. Basil of Caesarea argued that the names we use in describing things do not refer to the essence of things, but are notions that we make up to point to things that we cannot fully rationally grasp.[53] When we call the Father "un-generate" and the Son "generate," these names do not refer to the *essence* or nature of the Father and the Son, but to their *relations* as Father and Son. The Father and the Son share an ineffable and incomprehensible nature, but we can describe them as they relate to each other and to creation through the activities of God in the world. Language about God is, in this sense, always relational. Negative theology thus became an instrument in rejecting an approach to theology that was too rationalistic, while simultaneously affirming the creative ability and even right of human beings to make up names for God, even if God remains essentially ineffable.

This does not mean that negative theology equals irrationalism, or that theology is simply a product of human fantasy. There

52. Gregory of Nazianzus, *Oration* 28.5.

53. Basil of Caesarea, *Against Eunomius* 2.4.9–21.

is nothing contradictory in saying that God *in essence* can only be described through negative definitions, while God's *relations and works* can be described in positive terms. Rather than being a kind of irrationalism, for the Cappadocians negative theology was an alternative to both rationalism and irrationalism. When Neo-Arians claimed that trinitarianism was irrational with its claim that the Father and the Son share a common essence, negative theology made it possible to distinguish between essence and relations so that contradictions were avoided.

Basil's brother, Gregory of Nyssa, likewise insisted that God is essentially infinite and, as such, incomprehensible. We can refer to God's essence through negative theology, as we describe God in terms of what God is not. We cannot comprehend God in any final way, but this is exactly why we need to continuously make up new names for God so we do not get stuck with simplistic definitions of God. We do so, as Basil had also argued, by continuously inventing new language for God through a process of "conception" (*epinoia*). If we think we have finally comprehended the ineffable God, our concepts take on the form of idols, says Gregory. This was exactly what Eunomius brought about when claiming that the Father and the Son are respectively "un-generate" and "generate" in essence. For Eunomius, there was not much more than this to say about God. However, for Basil and Gregory, precisely because we cannot say anything definitive about the essence of the ineffable God, we need to keep talking about God so that we do not end up with the illusion that we have said everything there is to say. We cannot define things according to their essence.

Macrina the Younger, the sister of Gregory and Basil, explained in Gregory's dialogue *On the Soul and the Resurrection*, that "we either convey the idea of goodness by the negation of badness" or vice versa, which is to say that both must be defined through the negation of their opposite.[54] This dialectical method does not imply that the being of God or the good depends on what is opposite to God, the bad or evil, but only that our theological

---

54. Macrina according to Gregory of Nyssa, *On the Soul and the Resurrection* 37.

language always to some degree depends on implicit negations. In more technical terms, there is an asymmetry between ontology and epistemology: While the good is always primary to evil, which is nothing but the privation of good, we can only define the good indirectly by negating what is not good.

In other words, negative theology deflates our *concepts*, so that we do not confuse them with God. The Cappadocian view on language is expressed well in the saying that "concepts create idols, only wonder comprehends anything." This saying is often attributed to Gregory of Nyssa, although probably incorrectly, but even if he did not use these exact words, much suggests that he would have approved of the formula.[55]

The Infinite Good: More on Gregory of Nyssa

There is always more to say about God, exactly because we cannot adequately capture God in our finite definitions. Negative theology, however, is not just about language. It is just as much about how we relate to God. For Gregory and the other Cappadocians there was a deep spiritual significance to the fact that we can never fully grasp God with our finite minds.

As already suggested, at the heart of Cappadocian negative theology lies a novel notion of divine infinity. Greek philosophers had often seen infinity as either a matter of potentiality where there are no finite limits to how far we can count or perhaps as a synonym for chaos and disorder. Understood in these terms, infinity was quite irreconcilable with perfection. Gregory of Nyssa, however, insisted that God is essentially infinite and for this reason incomprehensible. For Gregory this was more than a technical matter, as negative theology also had a deep spiritual meaning. This is particularly clear from his later works, such as the commentaries

---

55. The saying is probably based on remarks made by Gregory in his *Life of Moses*. At one point, Gregory argues that "every concept which comes from some comprehensible image by an approximate understanding and by guessing at the divine nature constitutes an idol of God and does not proclaim God." See Gregory of Nyssa, *Life of Moses* 2.165.

On the Song of Songs and *The Life of Moses*. Developing a line of thought from Philo and Clement before him, Gregory read the story of Moses as a narrative about how spiritual progress is only possible by entering the "thick darkness." However, Gregory's more thoroughly apophatic form of negative theology goes further than Philo and Clement by emphasizing the infinity of God rather than, for example, God's oneness.

Gregory, in *The Life of Moses*, explains that when Moses entered the "thick darkness," he realized that what is divine is beyond all knowledge.[56] Moses had first experienced God as light in the burning bush, but as he learns more about God he encounters God in what Gregory famously describes as a "luminous darkness."[57] Although Moses initially experiences God as light, he eventually realizes that he can never fully comprehend the infinite God. There is always more to know. Moses finally learns that he can never see the face of God, but must follow God instead. To follow God wherever he might lead is to behold God, says Gregory.[58] This is because God is infinite. The good has no internal limit to its nature, but the good is only limited by its opposite. And since God is goodness in his very nature, the divine nature must also be thought of as unlimited and infinite.[59] It turns out that God is not, after all, completely without properties, since all things good—such as wisdom, life, righteousness, and so on—belong to God's essence. These things, however, *cannot be defined by human language* as they, due to God's infinity, always exceed our limited concepts.[60]

The infinity of the divine nature is why we are never done with God. When Gregory famously makes the paradoxical claim that "to see God is never to be fully satisfied in the desire to see

56. Gregory of Nyssa, *Life of Moses* 2.164.

57. Gregory of Nyssa, *Life of Moses* 2.163. Gregory seems to be closer to Philo than Clement in this, although he does not say that the darkness refers to the divine essence as such. What is called darkness by Scripture refers, says Gregory, to "the unknown and unseen." Gregory, *Life of Moses* 2.169.

58. Gregory of Nyssa, *Life of Moses* 2.252.

59. Gregory of Nyssa, *Life of Moses* 1.7.

60. See Radde-Gallwitz, *Basil of Caesarea, Gregory of Nyssa, and the Transformation of Divine Simplicity*, 200–212.

God," the point is that we must always reach out for what lies ahead of us. God grants what is desired in what is denied. Spiritual progress does not terminate in a static vision of God, but consists in a never-ending growth in the infinite good. The perfection of human nature consists in its very growth in goodness, says Gregory.[61] Nothing in human nature is exempt from change. But if this is the case, then neither is anything exempt from continuous perfection.

The Christian life is a journey that continues into eternity as expressed by the idea of *epektasis* ("reaching-out") that is often applied in reference to Gregory's idea of a never-ending growth in the good. When the apostle Paul in a letter had talked about forgetting what is behind and reaching out after what is ahead (Phil 3:13) the point was that since God is infinite, the good always lies ahead.[62] As a matter of negative theology, this also means that we must always be ready to negate our finite and limited notions of God and the good. We must do so in order to learn still more as had become clear from the debate with Eunomius who had made the mistake of thinking that he had arrived at a final definition of the divine nature.

It could be argued that in this way, Gregory anticipates modern ideas of perpetual change as a condition of life rather than something to escape from. Of course, change is bad if it results from sin, death, and decay, but there is also a good kind of change, or even death, made necessary by the infinity of the good. Once again in allusion to Paul, who elsewhere talked about how he "died daily" (1 Cor 15:31), Gregory argues that in order to have an ever-deeper relationship with the good, we need to continuously die in relation to what we have now. First of all, sin must be negated in order to reach life. The way to the tree of life goes through a negation of the tree of knowledge, as Gregory puts it in his commentary to The Song of Songs.[63] Our limited notions about the good must also be negated. Only in this way can we reach out for what lies ahead. Negative theology thus becomes a means of

61. Gregory of Nyssa, *Life of Moses* 1.10.
62. See Daniélou, *From Glory to Glory*, 305–7.
63. Gregory of Nyssa, *On the Song of Songs* 374.

opening oneself up to the infinity of God. Using negations is not a matter of denying perceived goodness, but negations are necessary for an ever deeper and richer experience of the good. This explains why, in contemporary moral philosophy, virtue ethicists, drawing on Gregory, have talked about "dialectical activities" as practices whose intrinsic value is only gradually revealed as we engage in them.[64] The good life is not just a matter of living up to certain moral standards, but of engaging still deeper with the good. In Gregory's case it is clear, however, that the notion of the good as somehow infinite cannot be separated from fundamental theological notions about the infinity of God.

Negative theology is always, first of all, a matter of theology. In addition, however, it turns out that negative theology also has a clear impact on *anthropology*. Philo of Alexandria had already connected the ineffability and incomprehensibility of God to the incomprehensibility of the human soul: "Why should we wonder that he, who is, cannot be apprehended by human beings when even the mind in each of us is unknown to us?" asked Philo.[65] Gregory follows suit: "Let those tell us who consider the nature of God to be within their comprehension, whether they understand themselves—if they know the nature of their own mind."[66] Being made in the image of God, human nature shows an exact likeness to God, but it does so by being incomprehensible like God. So Gregory explained in his treatise on the biblical narrative about the creation of humanity (Gen 1:27).

As the Russian theologian Nicolai Berdyaev would argue in the twentieth century, Gregory was the closest among the church fathers to formulate a truly *Christian* anthropology.[67] This is because the incomprehensibility and infinity of God shared in by human beings is also a matter of freedom. Freedom is a matter of sharing in God's autonomy, as Gregory's sister Macrina explained. Surrendering to God does not mean entering a slave-like

64. Brewer, *The Retrieval of Ethics*, 39.
65. Philo of Alexandria, *On the Change of Names* 7.10.
66. Gregory of Nyssa, *On the Making of Man* 11.2.
67. Berdyaev, *The Divine and the Human*, 22–23.

relationship to a master but is the coming up to a state that owns no master.[68] This again means not being confined by limited concepts of whatever a human being is said to be even while at the same time acknowledging the finitude of human nature. In other words, by reflecting the goodness of God, human beings are infinitely more than what they seem to be at first sight. While we have different bodily characteristics, in essence all human beings reflect God's infinity. As was the case with the divine persons, we can describe human beings in relation to their activities, but by its participation in human nature every human being infinitely transcends what can be comprehended. This apophatic anthropology also led Gregory to affirm the infinite value and equal dignity of all human beings. By reflecting the infinite but ineffable goodness of God, all human beings are infinitely valuable, even if we are finite beings.

Although the equal value of all human beings had long been a theme in Christianity, Gregory could use his negative theology in developing the theme even further and more poignantly. This became clear in his famous attacks on the institution of slavery, but also in a general criticism of human power and inequality.[69] Like Clement of Alexandria before him, Gregory emphasized the equal spiritual dignity of men and women, which naturally followed from the fact that our identities as human beings are equally grounded *in God*, rather than in material, bodily, or even social differences. This again exemplifies how negative theology was much more than simply a speculative practice but also had implications in real life.

Let's Not Talk Too Much about the Ineffable

To sum up: Often, negative theology is seen as resulting from the influx of Neoplatonism in Christian theology. However, the story is more complex, as suggested in the above. Philo of Alexandria might have already influenced Middle-Platonist philosophers like

---

68. Gregory of Nyssa, *On the Soul and the Resurrection* 101–5.

69. See Steenbuch, "A Christian Anarchist?" 573–88.

Alcinous with the notion of God's ineffability, while Clement of Alexandria, a generation before Plotinus, had already referred to God as the One that is infinite and for this reason cannot even be named "God" or "Being" properly. Rather than seeing early Christian theology as a passive recipient of novel philosophical ideas flowing in from the outside, it is probably more correct to see it as actively engaged in a more complex conversation with Jewish and Platonic thought, where Christian thinkers may even have influenced their pagan peers.

At the end of the fourth century, negative theology had developed from being a mostly polemical claim about the ineffability of God to being a fundamental vision of God and human nature with consequences for all aspects of life. Basically, negative theology as developed in the Neoplatonic and Christian traditions adds a new dimension to thought and language, breaking open our closed and finite concepts in a way that enables an unceasing wonder at the mystery of God, the world, and ourselves. This also explains why negative theology became a core element in the subsequent Christian tradition, especially in Eastern Orthodox theology.

The distinctions made by the Cappadocians, between God's infinite and incomprehensible essence on the one hand and God's comprehensible activities on the other, proved immensely influential in Greek-speaking Byzantine theology. The distinction was re-asserted by Maximus the Confessor around the sixth century and much later in the fourteenth century by the Greek monk Gregory Palamas in the so-called hesychast controversy. Barlaam of Seminara, an Italian convert to Eastern Orthodoxy, had argued that if God's activities were comprehensible, then they must be part of the created order, since God is altogether incomprehensible. Against this rather one-sided negative theology, Gregory Palamas asserted that while God is infinite and as such incomprehensible in essence, it is possible to experience and even comprehend God's uncreated activities insofar as they relate to us. To this day it is still discussed whether Palamas may have exaggerated the distinction between God's incomprehensible essence and God's comprehensible activities, since in Cappadocian theology God's essence may not have been completely void of properties such as goodness, wisdom, righteousness, and so on.[70] Even so, Palamas's clear distinction between the essence and activities of God has become a standard one in Eastern Orthodoxy.

Meanwhile, a less negative approach to theology would become foundational in the Latin-speaking West, primarily through the works of Augustine of Hippo (354–430), a younger contemporary of the Cappadocians. As Augustine argued, if something can be *called* "ineffable," it cannot be *completely* ineffable. For this reason, "God should not be said to be ineffable, for when this is said, something is said." But this is a contradiction in terms, argues Augustine.[71] Rather than trying to define God through negations, then, we should instead cease our attempts at defining what cannot be defined. Instead of trying to understand God through reason, we should relate to God in love.

It was, perhaps, this way of thinking that was echoed in the twentieth century when the Austrian philosopher Ludwig Wittgenstein famously concluded his *Tractatus Logico-Philosophicus* by saying that "whereof one cannot speak, thereof one must be silent." Wittgenstein's point was not that there is no such thing as the mystical, but that we can only point to it, not put it into words. Something similar seems to have been the case with Augustine. Even if Augustine at face value denied the benefits of negative theology altogether, it has been argued by some scholars that while negative theology is not an explicit approach in Augustine, it is, however, implicit in much of his thought.[72]

This perhaps explains why later theologians in the West did not necessarily see a problem in combining Augustine's thought with more explicit forms of negative theology. The fusion of Augustinian themes with Neoplatonic negative theology would, at any rate, eventually become central to medieval mysticism in the

---

70. Radde-Gallwitz, *Basil of Caesarea, Gregory of Nyssa, and the Transformation of Divine Simplicity*, 22–223.

71. Augustine, *De doctrina Christiana* 1.6.

72. See Carabine, *The Unknown God*, 259ff.

Latin West. We will now turn our attention to the development of this tradition.

II

Mystical Theology

The "Dark" Ages

O Trinity beyond being, beyond divinity, beyond goodness, and guide
of Christians in divine wisdom, direct us to the mystical summits
more than unknown and beyond light. There the simple, absolved, and
unchanged mysteries of theology lie hidden in the darkness beyond
light of the hidden mystical silence, there, in the greatest darkness, that
beyond all that is most evident exceedingly illuminates the sightless
intellects. There, in the wholly imperceptible and invisible, that beyond
all that is most evident fills to overflowing the sightless intellects with
the glories beyond all beauty. This is my prayer.

—Dionysius ("the Areopagite"), *Mystical Theology*

In the first chapter we saw how negative theology at the turn
of the fifth century appeared in a Christian version, as represented
especially by the theology of the Cappadocians, on the one hand,
and a pagan version, as represented by the Neoplatonic tradition,
on the other. These two streams would eventually come together in
the thought of an enigmatic theologian named Dionysius, whose

"mystical theology" with its themes of unknowing and divine darkness had a massive influence on a significant part of subsequent medieval theology and spirituality. Although "the Dark Ages" is often avoided today as a derogatory term for the period, the fascination with the divine darkness in negative theology does make it a fitting description of these streams of the period's intellectual landscape. In the West, the influence of Dionysius was most obvious in the works of John Eriugena, who translated Dionysius into Latin in the ninth century. A less explicit kind of negative theology also seems to have been the underlying assumption of Anselm of Canterbury's famous proof of God's existence. It reappears again in a Jewish context with Moses Maimonides in the twelfth century, while in the thirteenth century, a more moderate form was formulated by Thomas Aquinas. A rather radical version of negative theology appeared with Meister Eckhart and a number of lay movements inspired by his preaching. Although negative theology played a minor role in later scholastic theology, it did not die out in the late Middle Ages. It reappeared in the fifteenth century with Nicholas of Cusa, who stands out as one of the last great exponents of the Dionysian tradition. After the Middle Ages negative theology became, however, increasingly divorced from theoretical philosophy and theology, even if it lived on in forms of mystical spirituality.

The Darkness of Unknowing: (Pseudo-)Dionysius "the Areopagite"

When the apostle Paul delivered his famous speech about "the unknown God" at the Areopagus in Athens, the Acts of the Apostles relates how some of the listeners became followers of Paul (Acts 17:34). One of these was named Dionysius, which is how in the fifth or sixth century, Dionysius the Areopagite became the pseudonym for an otherwise unknown author often referred to today as Pseudo-Dionysius. This Dionysius was most likely a Syrian monk, heavily influenced by the Neoplatonic philosophy of Proclus of Athens (c. 412–85). Proclus, like Plotinus before him, had argued that "the One" can only be defined negatively. Where Plotinus talked about "removal" or "abstraction" (*aphairesis*), Proclus was more prone to talk about "negation" (*apophasis*), perhaps as a response to a recurrent debate on the philosophical use of negation.[1] However, Proclus also emphasized that even our negations must be removed from our definitions of "the One." The final union with "the One" happens in a mystical silence. It was this emphasis on the need for a final double negation that came to shape Dionysius's synthesis of Christian and Neoplatonic negative theology.[2]

Dionysius's *Mystical Theology* is among the most concise and poignant elaborations of negative theology of its kind. In the short treatise summing up the teachings from his earlier treatises, Dionysius not only develops his notion of "mystical theology," but also makes what is probably the first explicit distinction between the positive (*kataphatic*) and the negative (*apophatic*) ways of theology, the *via positiva* and the *via negativa*, as they would be later named in Latin.[3] As was the case with the Cappadocian theologians before Dionysius, these ways of talking of God were not contradictory or mutually exclusive, but rather different approaches to speaking about God who is beyond both positive and negative definitions.

Like negative theologians before him, Dionysius bases his theological speculations on the biblical narrative about Moses. When Moses met God in the thick darkness on the mountain, he learned that the mysteries of theology lie hidden in a mystical silence, a "darkness beyond light." Only through what Dionysius calls the "darkness of unknowing" can the theologian know God. That which is beyond knowledge must paradoxically be known by knowing nothing. Although we describe God as, for example, "good," "being," "one," and so on, Dionysius asserts that God, being the unique cause of all things, is beyond every affirmation, as well as every negation. God is neither darkness nor light, falsehood nor

---

1. See Jugrin, "The One Beyond Silence."

2. After Proclus, negative theology was further developed by Damascius, who went even further in his claims about a wholly ineffable principle beyond the One. Damascius, *Problems and Solutions about the First Principles* 2.1.4–13.

3. Dionysius, *On Mystical Theology* 2.

truth. This is why Moses can only know God through a kind of ignorance—not ignorance of the evil kind, of course, but a kind of superlative ignorance that transcends knowledge by going further than what ordinary knowledge can grasp.[4]

Dionysius adopts the Neoplatonic vocabulary of talking about God as "the One." As "the One," God is the principle of identity, but as such, God also contains the differences between created things. Unlike the tendency to speak of "the One" as beyond being, Dionysius does not describe God as simply beyond being altogether. Since God transcends all names, he is also beyond non-being, says Dionysius. God must ultimately be described as beyond being, as well as non-being.[5] In other words, God must be described as a *"hyper*-being." As later commentators of Dionysius would explain in more detail, our descriptions of God consist of three steps: First, we describe God using positive theology, as, for example "good" or "being." Then, through negative theology, we deny that God is simply like what we normally mean by "good" or "being." Finally, we affirm that God is beyond both positive and negative descriptions by calling God *hyper*-good or *hyper*-being.

As with earlier forms such next-level "hyper-phatic" negative theology should neither be considered as irrational nor outright contradictory, or simply absurd. The point is not that two contradictory statements about God can be simultaneously true in any direct sense. The point is rather to show that our concepts about God are only *partial* truths, metaphors that may point us to God, who is beyond contradictions. When we realize that two apparently contradictory statements about God are both true, this should remind us that none of them are exact descriptions of God. What we are dealing with is, in other words, what has sometimes been described as the logic of metaphor. Metaphors are not literally true, but they nevertheless convey some meaning.[6]

That this is the case becomes apparent when Dionysius talks about "unlike likenesses." An example of an "unlike likeness" is

4. Dionysius, *Epistle* 1.

5. Franke, *On What Cannot be Said, Vol. 1*, 20.

6. Turner, *Darkness of God*, 35–38.

when Psalm 78 speaks about God as waking from his sleep, and even as "drunk" (Ps 78:65).[7] Obviously God is neither sleeping nor drunk, Dionysius explains, but using such metaphors about God has the advantage that they should clearly be taken metaphorically because of their obvious unlikeness. That God is sleeping is a metaphor for his temporary removal from the objects of his providence, says Dionysius, while God's drunkenness is a metaphor for his overflowing and unlimited goodness.

As with earlier negative theologies, there is also an ethical or moral philosophical perspective to Dionysius's thinking. God is beyond all affirmations and negations, but this does not mean there is no significance in describing God as, for example, good rather than evil. God is the good beyond being, says Dionysius, echoing Socrates in Plato's *Republic*, even though Dionysius makes sure to explain that the good and being are not distinct things.[8] The term "good" describes everything that comes from God, but it can be used to describe things that are, as well as things that are not.

This notion of God as "the good beyond being" raises a problem. Affirming a classical doctrine in Christian theology, everything that exists has been created as good by God while evil does not have being. Evil is *non-being*, says Dionysius in his treatise *On the Divine Names*. However, even non-being (*to mē on*) participates in the good, insofar as it is ascribed by the abstraction of all properties to the God who is beyond being.[9] If God as the good is beyond being and can as such perhaps even be described as non-being, how is good then different from evil? Dionysius explains that while God is non-being as beyond being, the non-being of evil is a kind of privation of being. In a brilliant twist, Dionysius explains that evil results from creation's attempt to go beyond itself by destroying itself. Even "that which is not" desires "the

---

7. Dionysios, *On the Divine Names* 7.1.

8. Dionysius, *On the Divine Names* 5.1ff.

9. Dionysius, *On the Divine Names* 4.7.

all-transcendent good" and struggles, by its "denial of all things," to find rest in the good which transcends all being.[10]

In other words, our aim, rightly conceived, should not be to become like God in our own power, but to participate in God's goodness by abstracting from created things. This is just one of the ways in which Dionysius joins those before him who had been aware of the moral philosophical implications of negative theology. Dionysius, like Clement of Alexandria and Plotinus, also emphasizes how we should imitate God's simplicity. As the principle of unity beyond multiplicity, God is the source of true individuality. It is only by relating to the source of one's being that a person can become their true self. In distinction from Plotinus, however, but not unlike Clement and Gregory of Nyssa, for Dionysius, this individuation was not to be achieved alone, but through participation in the life of the church. The holy order (*hierarchia*) of the church is where diversity comes together in unity through liturgy. Again, it becomes clear how negative theology is not just a matter of abstract speculation, but is thoroughly connected to practice.

Nothing by Excellence: John Eriugena

As we have seen, negative theology originated to a high degree in the philosophical climate of Alexandria with all its urban eclecticism. Eventually, it would have an impact as far away as the British Isles. Missionaries had already brought the ascetic traditions of the Egyptian desert from the Eastern parts of the Roman empire to the most distant outskirts of the West. The philosophical elements of Eastern Christianity would again make an impact as Dionysius's Irish follower, John Scotus Eriugena (815–77), translated the works of Dionysius into Latin. This happened at the request of the French king Charles the Bald whose predecessor Louis the Pious had received a copy of Dionysius's writings from the Byzantine emperor. Dionysius's mystical theology was thus introduced to a Western audience. Moreover, Eriugena, who has been described as

---

10. Dionysius, *On the Divine Names* 4.3.

the most significant Irish intellectual of the early monastic period, not only translated Dionysius's works, but also made his own contributions to negative theology and philosophy, especially with his magnum opus *Periphyseon* or *On the Division of Nature*.[11]

Eriugena affirmed Dionysius's distinction between God, who, as the good, is beyond being on the one hand, and, on the other hand, evil, which as a privation lacks being. As expressed by Eriugena, the good is "nothing by excellence" (*nihil per excellentiam*) while evil is "nothing by privation" (*nihil per privationem*). Eriugena adds to Dionysius's understanding of God as beyond being by stating that if God is in this way "nothing," then creation from nothing could be understood as God creating from himself. To this he added, that if God is indeed beyond all differences, then as such, God cannot be absolutely different from the created world. Opposites only apply to things that come into being, but as the eternal beginning of all things God is beyond opposites. As such there can be nothing that is "different" (Eriugena uses the Greek *heterousion*) to God.[12] This is why God cannot be described using names that have opposites, such as "goodness" since "goodness" is opposed to "wickedness." We must, for this reason, instead describe God as *hyper*-being, *hyper*-good, and even *hyper*-God as if God was more than even himself. God can be opposed to neither life nor death, God is "larger than" both.

Eriugena explains that this way of describing God is only superficially affirmative, since it is implicitly negative in meaning. The idea that God is beyond opposites does, however, release negative theology from some of its more rigidly negative tendencies of making God completely distant to creation. Since God cannot be defined as "eternal" as opposed to "temporal," God must be understood as *beyond* eternal. But as such God cannot be opposed to created, temporal beings. God is, in other words, *so* different that he is *beyond difference* itself.

As diffused through all things, God is made all things in all things (*in omnibus omnia*), says Eriugena, as well as nothing in

11. Moran, *The Philosophy of John Scotus Eriugena*.

12. Eriugena, *Periphyseon* 457dff.

nothing (*in nullo nullam*).[13] Creation is perceived by Eriugena as divine self-manifestation, where God moves from darkness and ignorance to light and self-knowledge. The ineffable and incomprehensible God is made comprehensible indirectly through creation. What is understood and sensed in creation is nothing but the manifestation of the hidden, and the affirmation of the negated (*negati affirmatio*).[14] In a way, God can even be said to create himself in creation. Eriugena explains that God's creative nature permits nothing outside of itself, because nothing can exist outside of God. However, he also importantly adds that even if creation is contained in God, God is still apart from creation because he is beyond being.[15]

It should be clear by now that some very radical claims follow from the idea of God as beyond being or, in other words, God as "nothing." Some have to do with the knowledge of God, while others have to do with anthropology. Knowledge has to do with knowing things as "something," says Eriugena, but since God is infinite, God is not something that can be known.[16] Because God does not have the status of a "what," not even God himself knows what he is. This does not, of course, mean that God is ignorant, but only that God does not know himself through discursive reasoning. Moreover, like theologians before him, Eriugena was aware how a negative theology of this kind led to a negative anthropology that had implications for how we perceive human beings. Since human beings are made in the image of God, they share the divine characteristics, but because God is infinite and, for this reason, does not "know" himself as "something," this also applies to humans. In other words, human beings are not "things." Reflecting God's infinity, human nature is ineffable and incomprehensible, as was also affirmed by Gregory of Nyssa already in the fourth century.[17]

---

13. Eriugena, *Periphyseon* 668c.

14. Eriugena, *Periphyseon* 633a–b.

15. Eriugena, *Periphyseon* 675c.

16. Eriugena, *Periphyseon* 589b–c.

17. Eriugena, *Periphyseon* 919c.

Eriugena radicalizes this line of thought. We do not know ourselves in essence, but only through what we do and create.

Ideas like these became important in the subsequent mystical theology of the Latin West. However, even if Eriugena made sure to carefully distinguish between God and creation, he would eventually end up being condemned for the pantheism that was allegedly implicit in his thinking. Nevertheless, through his translations, the Dionysian tradition made an impact in Western European theology through the Middle Ages, with influential names such as the Jewish philosopher Moses Maimonides and the Christian thinkers Albert the Great and Thomas Aquinas as the most prominent examples. However, before invoking Thomas, we will take a look at how negative theology might implicitly have been present in the great Italian-English theologian, Anselm of Canterbury.

"That Than Which No Greater Can Be Conceived": Anselm of Canterbury

Anselm of Canterbury (1033–1109) was an Italian-born Benedictine monk and philosopher, who held the office of Archbishop of Canterbury from 1093 until his death in 1109. While famous for his theory of the atonement, Anselm is arguably best known for his so-called ontological proof of God. Often, this argument for the existence of God is presented as a rationalistic attempt at deducing the necessity of God's existence simply by analyzing the meaning of the concept "God." It turns out, however, that this characterization should be balanced by an awareness of the negative theology that frames not just Anselm's arguments but also most classical arguments for the existence of God. Before engaging further with Anselm we will have to take a few steps back in time.

The apostle Paul, in his epistle to the Romans, had famously claimed that "the invisible things of God can be seen from the foundation of the world" (Rom 1:20). The point was moral in character: since we can all see that God must have made the world, we are also morally culpable for not honoring God as creator. Whatever Paul's precise point was in making this claim about

45

the "invisible things of God," his reasoning did not make early Christian theologians think that God *in his essence* could become rationally known, for example by a "natural theology" that derives certain insights about God through observations of nature. Most theologians agreed that creation reveals the existence of God, as well as his goodness and wisdom. However, God is still essentially ineffable and incomprehensible. At one point, Gregory of Nyssa even interpreted Paul's words on "the invisible things of God" as referring to the economy of salvation—the incarnation, death, and resurrection of God's Word in Jesus Christ—that had been proclaimed since the "foundation of the world," which Gregory took to mean the foundation of the church.[18] As mentioned above, Gregory of Nazianzus similarly explained that while there may be good reasons for believing that God has created the world, this knowledge does not reveal God's ineffable nature.

This perspective, shaped by a more or less implicit negative theology, is often overlooked when we deal with attempts at developing proofs for the existence of God during the Middle Ages. Returning to Anselm, a good example is his *Proslogion* or *Discourse on the Existence of God*. Later dubbed the "ontological argument" by Immanuel Kant, at first sight, Anselm's proof seems to derive God's existence from a reflection on "ontology" (a theory of being). In his discourse, Anselm defines God as the "being than which no greater can be conceived" and argues that as such, God must exist since existence would indeed be a feature of such a being. Existence is, in other words, implicit in the notion of God, which is why we cannot conceive of God as not existing.

This seems to place Anselm far from the Neoplatonic tradition that, like Dionysius and Eriugena, typically described God as beyond being. From this perspective "being" is surely not a part of the definition of God. Theologians in the twentieth century have, however, emphasized how Anselm's discourse was not an attempt to prove the existence of God for outsiders, but rather a reflection on the content of faith for the faithful, thereby presupposing some

18. Gregory, *On the Song of Songs* 13, 384–385.

idea of God.[19] Moreover, Anselm is, in fact, not simply saying that God must necessarily exist because he exists as an idea in our minds. Rather, the idea of "that than which nothing greater can be conceived" points beyond itself towards the God beyond anything we can imagine.[20] Since it can be conceived that there is something that is greater than what can be conceived, God must be greater than what can be conceived.

In this there is arguably an apophatic element. We can think of something beyond what can be thought, but only be negating thought itself. When we think of such a being we do not think in terms of definitions but rather give up our definitions of God. It is the very possibility of negative theology that makes it possible to talk of God as more than what can be captured by our definitions of God. In other words, Anselm begins with a "definition" of God requiring us to acknowledge divine "existence" but eventually arrives at a much more apophatic notion of God as beyond every definition.

From the perspective of negative theology, Anselm's point seems to be that God, as that than which nothing greater can be conceived, is *even more than can be conceived*, and that God, for this very reason, must also "exist" outside the limited concepts that we are able to imagine. God is not just an idea in our minds, but God escapes the narrow confines of our limited minds. For this reason, as argued by Jean-Luc Marion, Anselm's proof may just as well be termed "non-ontological."[21] The existence of God is not deduced, that is, from a theory of being (onto-logy).

When Anselm in subsequent chapters goes on to talk about God as unapproachable light, stressing the ineffability and transcendence of God, this also suggests that his discourse on the existence of God cannot be adequately understood independently of some sort of negative theology. This is not because God is completely remote or absent, but because God, as in earlier theology, is the being from which everything that exists derives its being by

19. See Barth, *Fides quaerens intellectum.*

20. Anselm, *Proslogion* 15.

21. Marion, "Is the Ontological Argument Ontological?"

participation. In God we move and have our being, as Paul explained in his sermon on the Areopagus, but this is exactly why God cannot be approached as any other being: "O supreme and inaccessible light . . . how far You are from me, who am so near to You!" exclaims Anselm.[22] God exists before and transcends all things, even eternal things.[23] In this way, God can hardly be considered a being comparable to other beings.

To be sure, Anselm is not saying, like Dionysius and Eriugena, that God is beyond being, but such an understanding is at least possible to the degree that God in Anselm's "definition" can be thought of as more than what can be conceived. This again suggests that when balanced by a healthy negative theology, so-called proofs of God's existence should not be taken as attempts at fleshing out a closed, rational system that makes the mysteries of God intellectually comprehensible. On the contrary, arguments for the existence of God should make us open to the mystery that lies at the heart of our existence.

God Is One: Moses Maimonides

As mentioned in the first chapter, the beginnings of negative theology can to a great extent be traced back to the fusion of Jewish theology with Hellenic philosophy by Philo of Alexandria in the first century AD. Even though Philo did not win much support in the Jewish community of his time, his thinking on a wide variety of theological topics became influential in early Christian philosophy. Only much later do we find examples of Jewish philosophy taking up the cue from Philo's negative theology. The most prominent example appears in the twelfth century with Moses Maimonides (1138–1204).

Moses Maimonides was born in Cordoba in Spain, but he was exiled to Egypt when the Islamic authorities began forcing the conversion of Jews and Christians in Spain. Writing in Arabic,

22. Anselm, *Proslogion* 16.

23. Anselm, *Proslogion* 20.

Maimonides published his grand theological work the *Guide of the Perplexed* in 1190. In this book, Maimonides argued in line with traditional forms of negative theology that the positive names we use to describe God are either (a) implicit negations expressing what God is not or (b) descriptions of God's works in the world.[24] Thus, when we say that "God is good," this is equivalent to saying either that *God is not evil* or that *God is the cause of goodness in creation.*

In this, Maimonides echoed the Cappadocians, who had also argued that we can define God either through negations or by describing God's activities in the world (though for the Cappadocians, God's activities were arguably more than simply the works or effects of God). To Maimonides, God is radically distinct from the world, and can as such only be known through his effects. This is affirmed, argues Maimonides, when Ecclesiastes says that "God is in heaven and you are on earth. Therefore, let your words be few" (Eccl 5:1). Silence is, for this reason, preferable to praise.[25] While he agrees a long way with, for example, Gregory of Nyssa here, Maimonides unsurprisingly rejects the trinitarian theology of Christianity. God is absolutely one, though even God's oneness must be understood in apophatic terms as saying that God has no equal.[26] That God is truly "one" implies the absolute denial of any plurality in God whatsoever. It also means, in line with Plato's *Parmenides*, that God has no essential attributes at all.

Not surprisingly, Maimonides takes up the story of Moses from Exodus, as many negative theologians before him. What Moses comprehended has never been grasped as well by anyone else before or since, says Maimonides. When Moses sought to know God as God really is, on the one hand, and through his attributes, on the other, this request was acceded as Moses was made aware that *the attributes of God* are *his works*, while also being taught that *God cannot be comprehended as he really is.* To know the attributes of God is equal to knowing the works of God in creation.

24. Moses Maimonides, *Guide of the Perplexed* 1.58.
25. Moses Maimonides, *Guide of the Perplexed* 1.59.
26. Moses Maimonides, *Guide of the Perplexed* 1.54.

Maimonides further argues that when God is said to be, for example, "existing," "living," or "powerful," this should not be taken in the same sense as when applied to human beings. The difference between human beings and God is not simply a matter of magnitude or quantity, as if God has existence in the same manner as human beings, only to a quantitatively greater extent.[27] Importantly, as a result of God's lack of attributes, "existence" is not something that God can have or not have. God's essence *is* God's existence, says Maimonides, though it cannot be defined in positive terms.[28] All the attributes of God's essence can be reduced to a single, undifferentiated principle that can, however, only be apprehended through negative predicates.[29]

That all positive predicates for God are derived from his works can be proved by the fact that all names for God in the Scriptures are derived from verbs, Maimonides argues.[30] There is, however, one exception, since the name YHWH was invented specifically for God. When we abstract all attributes from God, this is the explicit name that is left. While Maimonides in many ways seems to agree with Philo of Alexandria here, they may seem to disagree on this, as Philo can sometimes say that even God's name is only a substitute name derived from his existence. At other times Philo did argue, however, that "The One Who Is" (Exod 3:14) is God's proper name, although since *only* God "is" in the proper sense, this name must at any rate be considered exclusive to God.[31] Philo's point was, at any rate, that since God is being itself, God is ineffable. Maimonides takes this point further in a more systematic and developed negative theology. That God has a proper name does not mean that God's essence can be defined or comprehended in any way. When it is prophesied in Zechariah that the name of YHWH one day will be one, this means that God will eventually only be known by the one name which designates his Godhead.

27. Moses Maimonides, *Guide of the Perplexed* 1.56.

28. Moses Maimonides, *Guide of the Perplexed* 1.57.

29. Moses Maimonides, *Guide of the Perplexed* 1.58.

30. Moses Maimonides, *Guide of the Perplexed* 1.61.

31. Carabine, *The Unknown God,* 209.

This will happen when people come to realize that the plurality of attributes of God are derived from either verbs or negative definitions and that only the name YHWH is God's proper name.

There is thus an eschatological perspective to negative theology in Maimonides's thought, one that would later reappear in twentieth-century Jewish thinkers such as Franz Rosenzweig and Walter Benjamin. After Maimonides, forms of negative theology became an important part of the kabbalistic tradition where the term *Ein Sof* came to refer to God's infinite and nameless being. Negative theology also came to play a role in Islamic philosophy with Ibn al-Arabi, who in turn became influential in later Sufi mysticism. The mainstream of negative theology in Western thought culminated, however, in Dominican thinkers like Thomas Aquinas and Meister Eckhart, and later Nicholas of Cusa, who were all to some degree indebted to Moses Maimonides and the Dionysian tradition.

"As to the Unknown": Thomas Aquinas

It was not only the Jewish tradition that received and developed further the negative theology present in Moses Maimonides. It was also discussed by Christian theologians like the famous Dominican Thomas Aquinas (1225–74), who would moderate some of Maimonides's more radical claims. Often perceived as one of the major proponents of natural theology, Thomas is equally famous for introducing Aristotelian philosophy into Christian theology. While this has sometimes given Thomas the reputation of being an intellectualist who wanted to encompass everything in a comprehensive system, such characterization overlooks the fact that Thomas had a high veneration for traditional negative theology. In fact, Thomas ascribes great authority to Dionysius, quoting him more than 1,700 times in his *Summa Theologica*.

Just as with Anselm, the Dionysian heritage should be borne in mind when considering Thomas's proofs of the existence of God. In his "Five Ways," Thomas expanded on the classical arguments for God's existence based on observations of the nature of the world.

Though the proofs of the five ways are more "empirical" in kind than Anselm's, they share his concern to show that our language only points to God by pointing beyond itself. We know God in the sense that the *effects* of God are demonstrated to us, says Thomas, but even by revelation, in this life, we cannot know what God is *in himself*. We can find a trace of God in all creatures, though a trace only shows that someone has passed by, and not who this is, as Thomas puts it with allusions to the story of Moses.[32] As such, he affirms the traditional concerns of negative theology. Thomas concludes with a paraphrase of Dionysius when saying that in this life, we are united to God "as to the unknown," since we cannot know what God is, even if we can know something about God through his effects and revelation.[33] As with Anselm, Thomas's proofs are not so much attempts at confining God to a convenient box in our theological system as they are attempts, so to speak, at opening up cracks so that the light can shine in. Or perhaps a more adequate metaphor may be that created beings themselves reflect the light from the incomprehensible God in whose being they participate, even if God cannot, for this reason, be made comprehensible.

Thomas's teacher at the university in Paris, Albert the Great (d. 1280), had also engaged with the Dionysian tradition in his commentaries on Dionysius's works. Albert affirmed the basic ideas in Dionysius's approach, explaining that God can be adequately described neither by positive nor negative definitions. However, the negative definitions are more precise than the positive. This is not because God lacks anything, of course, but because God is beyond any definition.[34] Following Aristotle and in distinction from the Dionysian tradition, Albert, however, defined God as the *first* being, rather than as *beyond* being. This approach was taken up by Thomas, who like Albert, was critical towards the Neoplatonic definition of God as completely beyond being. Instead, Thomas made sure to affirm the definition of God as "The One Who Is" in

32. Thomas Aquinas, *Summa theologiae* 1.45.7.
33. Thomas Aquinas, *Summa theologiae* 1.12.13.
34. Albert, *On Dionysius' Mystical Theology* 5.

the traditional translation of God's self-description to Moses in the Septuagint's Exodus 3:14.

Dionysius, Thomas admits, is not wrong in saying that we have no words that can describe God in any adequate or direct way. It is not enough, however, to say that a definition like "God is good" is simply equivalent to saying that "God is not evil." As a proponent of this view, Thomas explicitly mentions Moses Maimonides. In distinction to this, Thomas argues that it is not enough to understand positive definitions of God simply as implicit negations. If God is "good," then this must surely mean more than just saying that God is not evil or that God is the cause of good things, as if God was not in himself good. What we call "goodness" in creatures must pre-exist in God on a higher level, says Thomas. This is how we must understand the point of Dionysius's method. By stating that God is *"hyper-*good," we have a way of saying that God is good, but in a *higher* sense than how we usually conceive of goodness. God is not simply "good" in the usual senses, although the term "not good" is, of course, also non-applicable to God. That God is good in a higher sense is not just a matter of *quantity*, as if God were good like the good things we know, only *many times better*. Rather, the point is that God must be good, being the source of all goodness, although in a quite *different and truer* sense than our normal use of the word. Likewise, God is not beyond being, but as the source of all that is, God is being in a higher sense than created things. Created beings only have their being in a derived sense by participation in being itself, which is why God is being in a way that is both similar and dissimilar to created beings.

In other words, for Thomas, theological language is *analogical*. When human words are applied to God, they do not mean exactly the same thing as when they are applied to creatures, nor do they mean something completely different. In more technical language, words are not used of God and creatures univocally (i.e., in the same sense) nor equivocally (i.e., in a completely different sense), but analogically (i.e., in a related but different sense). Implicit negations in our definitions of God keep our theological language from collapsing into ordinary language, so to speak. A proper dose of negative theology ensures that we do not mistakenly consider our normal language adequate when describing God.

God is not just a thing among other things, albeit an infinitely greater and better thing. Talk of God as "the first cause" should not be understood in the temporal and spatial sense that God is simply like the first efficient cause in a series of events leading to the world as we know it, like a finger pushing over the first domino in a cascading line of dominos.[35] That would make God an object in the world acting like other objects in the world. This is also why Thomas's proofs of the existence of God do not end in a grand theory of all things, but instead open up a mystery.[36] Creation points beyond itself, but not in a way that makes it possible to grasp God as though God was just a part of a comprehensive worldview. Rather, creation speaks of an infinite mystery, by pointing to the divine source of being.

In this way, Thomas formulated a moderate middle way, combining affirmative and negative theology. Soon after Thomas, however, this moderate approach would give way, on the one hand, to the more positivistic theology of John Duns Scotus (1265–08), whose teachings on the "univocity" of being would challenge Thomas's analogical understanding of language, and, on the other hand, more radical forms of mystical theology.

"Let us pray to God that we may be free of God!": Marguerite Porete and Meister Eckhart

In the fourteenth century, new and radical movements arose around the Rhineland between Germany and France. One of the most remarkable exponents of these movements was the French mystic Marguerite Porete (1250–1310). We know little about her life, but her beliefs were recorded in her book *The Mirror of Simple Souls*. Here Marguerite took up themes from the Dionysian tradition and explained how the human soul must in some

35. Richard Dawkins, according to David Bentley Hart, makes this mistake in his criticism of Thomas. Hart, *The Experience of God*, 21–22.

36. Denys Turner, "Apophaticism, Idolatry and the Claims of Reason."

sense be annihilated in order to remain in what she describes as a "pure nothingness without thought." God is only known, loved, or praised by creatures insofar as we admit that God cannot, in fact, be known, loved, or praised by creatures.[37] Since God is always greater than what can be said, everything we say or write about God really amounts to lying more than speaking the truth. God can, in other words, only be approached in a silence beyond language where the human soul forgets itself.

This resembles the traditional Neoplatonic notion that we are only united to the good to the degree that God is no longer conceived as an object of thought. The union with God that is sought in this way requires that we cannot, conversely, conceive of ourselves as subjects. We are, in other words, to become "nothing." This is not, of course, what we today would call "nihilism" or a rejection of all positive values. In Marguerite's writings the Neoplatonic, apophatic approach to theology was combined with what is sometimes called *Minnemystik* with its more Augustinian and positive emphasis on love. True love for God can only be attained, however, insofar as we acknowledge the inadequacy of our own love. As Marguerite famously says in her book: "I have said that I will love Him. I lie, for I am not. It is He alone who loves Me."[38] The emphasis on the need for divine grace in love from the Augustinian tradition here join hands with elements of negative theology.

Similar mystical forms of negative theology gained ground in popular movements such as the Beguines, a women's lay movement that stressed the imitation of Christ but without taking formal vows. In the German vernacular, thoughts akin to Marguerite's were developed further in the preaching of Eckhart of Hochheim (c. 1260–1328), also known as Meister Eckhart. A Dominican like Thomas Aquinas, Eckhart was drawing more heavily on Moses Maimonides and Dionysius, and, perhaps under the influence of Marguerite Porete, his theology was more radical in its claims about the nature of the human soul and God. Eckhart did affirm, along with Thomas, that God is the highest being, but

37. Marguerite Porete, *The Mirror of Simple Souls* 95.

38. Marguerite Porete, *The Mirror of Simple Souls* 122.

he also added that God, being simple and without differences, must be conceived as "nothing" at the same time. Eckhart seems to have agreed with Duns Scotus about the univocity of being, since "being" always means the same thing when applied to God or creatures. For Eckhart, however, this meant that if God is being then creation is nothing and *vice versa*.[39] For Eckhart, as for John Eriugena before him, this also leads to the idea that in a way, being and nothingness are two sides of the same coin in God. This has wide-ranging implications for how we conceive of the soul's relation to God.

Eckhart relates how the light that is said to have blinded the apostle Paul (Acts 9:8) was God's "true light," which is, in fact, "nothing." In seeing nothing, Paul saw "the divine nothing."[40] God is "nothing," says Eckhart, although not in the sense of having no being at all, but in the sense of not being *this* or *that* in terms of a being that we can speak of.[41] God is the "nameless nothingness" beyond being. But for this reason, those who want to see God must first be reduced to nothing themselves.[42] Eckhart describes God as "light," but God hides in a darkness that makes him incomprehensible.[43] What we call "God" is not the God that hides in darkness. The true God is beyond darkness, as well as light. When God described himself to Moses as "The One Who Is" (Exod 3:14) the point was, says Eckhart, that God is the denial of all names, as God is altogether nameless.[44] The end or aim of being is the darkness of the hidden divinity where the light shines.

God is "the hidden God," as described by the prophet Isaiah (Isa 45:15). However, God does not hide far away from us. On the contrary, God hides in "the ground of the soul," says Eckhart. God's ground and the ground of the soul are in some way one. For

---

39. Moss, "The Problem of Evil in the Speculative Mysticism of Meister Eckhart," 35ff.

40. Meister Eckhart, *Sermon 71*.

41. Meister Eckhart, *Sermon 82*.

42. Meister Eckhart, *Sermon 39*.

43. Meister Eckhart, *Sermon 22*.

44. Meister Eckhart, *Sermon 15*.

this reason, we do not find God by seeking God as if God was not close to us. The more we seek God, the less we find God. Only by seeking God nowhere or by not seeking God will we find God.

This is the background for some of Eckhart's provocative statements that must have been quite shocking to his audience. In a famous sermon on Jesus's beatitude about being "poor in spirit" (Matt 5.3), Eckhart explains that insofar as God is thought of as God, then God is not the perfect end of created beings.[45] We cannot be united to God as long as God is conceived of as an object. This is because, for Eckhart, God is beyond what can be thought and imagined. As a culmination of this line of thought Eckhart famously encourages his listeners to pray to be rid of their ideas of God: "So therefore, let us pray to God that we may be free of God." The point is not just, however, that we should be freed from our wrong conceptions of God. Rather, what Eckhart is saying is that God must altogether cease to be a distant object of thought.

God must become a subject that acts through us spontaneously. Only when we stop trying to understand and comprehend God as a different object to ourselves can God act freely in and through us. Everything that ever comes from God is directed into "pure activity," says Eckhart. We should be so free of knowing that we are unaware that God lives in us. This is also why Eckhart can explain that as long as we have the will to do God's will, it is not really God's will, but our own will, that we are seeking to carry out. Only by spontaneously doing God's will can we do the will of God. This is the meaning of being "poor in spirit," argues Eckhart. Poverty of spirit keeps us free of God so that God can work in the soul as he pleases.

Eckhart makes an important distinction between God as "Godhead" (*Gottheit*) and God (*Gott*) as "God." Roughly speaking, this is a distinction between God as absolute and God in relation to the world. God as "God" appears to be both good and evil, since opposites in the world are contained in each other, like light and darkness. But God as "Godhead" is beyond good and evil. The human will perceives God as goodness, but since God is without

45. Meister Eckhart, *Sermon* 52.

name, God cannot be conceived as "good" as such. Since "goodness" does not apply to God as "Godhead" we can, Eckhart argues, even say that human beings are "better" than God.[46] God can also be said to be beyond love and, as such, God can be described as "unlovable." God, says Eckhart, can only be loved in an unspiritual sense as non-God, non-spirit, non-person, non-image. This means that God cannot be loved in accordance with our dual concepts of God, but, echoing Neoplatonism, only as "the One" separated from all duality. "In that One," says Eckhart, "we should eternally sink down out of something into nothing."

The fact that God is beyond good and evil does not mean, of course, that there is no difference between good and evil, virtue and vice. For Eckhart, sin and evil must be conceived as a willful upholding of a false distinction between God and creation rather than letting oneself be one with God. Becoming one with God is only possible through detachment, the highest of all virtues, described by Eckhart as a state free of relations to things. For the same reason, Eckhart can also explain that we do not find God in "ways." Whoever is seeking God in ways, says Eckhart, may find ways, but will be losing God. In other words, there is no spiritual "method" that can teach us to attain unity with God by engaging in specific practices. This is why Eckhart can also argue that those who possess God in the right way, possess God in all places, whether on the street, in the company of others, in church, or in a cell.

The teachings of Meister Eckhart and Marguerite Porete may be conceived of as a reaction to a still more positive and intellectualistic approach to theology in late medieval scholasticism. As such it should come as no surprise that their teachings were met with suspicion if not outright hostility. Marguerite Porete was tragically condemned as a heretic and burned for her writings. In her *The Mirror of Simple Souls* she had argued that the soul's love for God must transcend and even leave behind the moral virtues. For critics, such teachings led to a dangerous disregard for the moral law. Eckhart was luckier, although some of his teachings

---

46. Meister Eckhart, *Sermon* 83.

were condemned posthumously. While Eckhart's claim that God can be possessed in all places and not just in particular "ways" may not in itself seem very controversial, it too might have contributed to sparking movements such as the Brethren of the Free Spirit, who became known and condemned for their allegedly anti-clerical views and moral lawlessness.

Teachings similar to Marguerite's and Eckhart's lived on in the fourteenth century in English mystic literature such as the anonymous *The Cloud of Unknowing* and Julian of Norwich's *Revelations of Divine Love*. On the continent it was expressed in less radical forms by John Tauler and Henry Suso in the Dominican order. Through writings such as the anonymous *Theologia Deutsch,* this tradition would eventually make an impact with reverberations in important parts of the Protestant Reformation and beyond.

Learned Ignorance: Nicholas of Cusa

While negative theology in the latter part of the Middle Ages flourished in mystical settings, in Nicholas of Cusa (1401–64) it found a new spokesman capable of combining the mystical side of negative theology with the intellectual and speculative side. Nicholas explains how he had originally received a revelation that was to shape his whole way of thinking about God, humanity, and the universe. This happened on a ship heading homewards to Italy from Greece. Coming to him in a way he described as "a celestial gift from the Father of Lights," this made Nicholas realize that truth can only be known through what he describes as a "learned ignorance." Such learned ignorance, says Nicholas, is arrived at "by transcending those incorruptible truths that can be humanly known."

Nicholas himself relates how he came to this realization in a letter attached to his great work *On Learned Ignorance.* From other sources, we know that before boarding the ship, Nicholas had been in Constantinople as an ambassador for the pope to win the support of the Greek Church for a union council in Italy. Since the great schism in 1054, the Roman Catholic Church and the Greek Orthodox Church had excommunicated each other, officially due to dogmatic controversies on the details of the Nicene Creed. Nicholas was part of the effort to bridge the ecclesiastical divide that scarred Christian civilization. For Nicholas, there was a deep connection between negative theology and the practical pursuit of unity in diversity, as will be explained more fully below.

A central notion in Nicholas's *On Learned Ignorance* is the idea of God as the "coincidence of opposites."[47] As claimed by earlier negative theology in the Neoplatonic and Dionysian traditions, God is beyond both affirmation and negation. Nicholas takes this idea further by applying it to the nature of infinity. He reminds us that there is no proportion between the infinite and the finite. Infinite truth is always greater than anything we can comprehend. The human intellect can always attain further precision in comprehending truth, and so, the only way to access infinite truth is through a kind of thinking that acknowledges our basic incomprehension of truth. As an illustration, Nicholas describes the human intellect as a polygon that grows to become still more like a circle as the number of angles increases, though it will never actually become a circle.

Nicholas joins this line of thinking with his notion of the "coincidence of opposites." He explains this in terms of "the maximum" and "the minimum" by again using examples from geometry. For example, the maximum line can be understood as maximally straight and minimally curved, while infinite curvature can conversely be understood as infinite straightness. Again there is a theological point, since in God the minimum coincides with the maximum. Opposites apply only to things that are greater and lesser, but God is above all opposition. God is, as such the "coincidence of opposites." Dionysius the Areopagite hinted at this truth, says Nicholas, when he asserted that God is above all affirmations while being the unique cause of all things.

Nicholas developed his negative theology further in a short dialogue entitled *On the Hidden God*.[48] In this dialogue, a pagan stops by a praying Christian to ask who the Christian

47. Nicholas of Cusa, *On Learned Ignorance.*

48. Nicholas of Cusa, *On the Hidden God.*

is worshiping. The pagan is understandably surprised when the Christian answers "I do not know!" But as the Christian explains, this is exactly why he worships God. It makes better sense to worship something that you know you do not know than pretending to know something that you are actually ignorant of. However, the Christian in Nicholas's dialogue knows this much: that nothing of the things he knows is God. I know that whatever I know is not God, he explains the baffled pagan. God is beyond every name. This is where the Neoplatonic heritage becomes clearest. God is even beyond "nothing" to the degree that nothing has the name "nothing."[49] This does not mean that God can then be conceived of as "something." God is beyond nothing and something, for nothing obeys God in order that something can be made. This is because God in his omnipotence makes not-being pass into being and being pass into not-being.

When reading Nicholas's dialogue we easily get the feeling that he is writing with tongue in cheek. This is not least the case when the Christian declares that God is neither nothing or not-nothing but the source of all the beginnings of being and of not-being. To be sure, the confused pagan in Nicholas's dialogue repeats what the Christian had just said. The Christian, however, replies with just another paradox: It was true what I said before, he says, but it is also true when I deny it now. All these paradoxes follow from the fact that God is beyond what we call truth too. Being truth itself, God cannot be known. This has to do with the character of truth: Truth itself is not something we can know. It is rather the medium, so to speak, that enables us to know all particular truths.[50] This is not unlike the way that vision, not itself being color, is nevertheless the medium through which we perceive color. Truth, like vision, affirms the being of all that is present in it, but it is itself not some "thing." Although God in this way precedes all truths, this does not mean, however, that God is "other" than truth, since "otherness" cannot be ascribed to God.

---

49. Nicholas of Cusa, *On the Hidden God* 11.
50. Nicholas of Cusa, *On the Hidden God* 14.

These thoughts were further developed in Nicholas's dialogue *On the Not-Other*.[51] As the principle of identity beyond all differences, God is not just the "other" but also the "not-other." Everything that exists is, by being itself, "not-other" than itself, but everything derives this feature from God. However, if God is the "not-other," the difference between God and the world is, to some degree, illusory. This does not, however, amount to a pantheism, where God and the universe are simply identical. Being quite different from all the differences that we experience in the world, God is the infinite reality that continuously upholds creation with all its differences and identities. In his book on learned ignorance, these ideas had already led Nicholas to some quite remarkable conclusions about the nature of the universe. All beings are enfolded in God's oneness, while God is unfolded in time and space as the created universe. As such, God is the center of the universe, but since God is infinite, there can be no fixed center. Rather, Nicholas argues, the center of the universe is relative to the observer, thereby perhaps even anticipating Galileo's dismissal of the geo-centric worldview.

Nicholas of Cusa's philosophy of science is closely linked to his negative theology. We cannot know the truth in any final and adequate way but must continue to make qualified guesses to understand still more. Nicholas was highly interested in matters of mathematics, geometry, and astronomy, but like other proponents of negative theology, he simultaneously drew spiritual and moral conclusions from his negative theology. Nicholas partly affirmed the traditional ascetic ideals that followed from negative theology. In addition to this, however, he was more aware than most of how the idea of God as the good beyond all affirmations and negations could also have a political significance. In his book on learned ignorance, Nicholas had already explained that God has made us incapable of judging which nations are more excellent than others in the world, in order that we should admire each other while remaining content with ourselves and our native lands and customs. This is the idea of learned ignorance as applied to politics and

51. Nicholas of Cusa, *On the Not-Other.*

culture. The purpose is unity and peace without envy, says Nicholas. This is only possible for those who reign with the peace of God that surpasses all understanding (Phil 4:6). For Nicholas, in other words, a high ideal of unity in diversity naturally followed from the notion of God as "the One" that is the source of both unity and multiplicity in the world.

This is particularly clear in Nicholas's dialogue *On the Peace of Faith* from 1453. In this text, written the same year that Christian Constantinople fell and was captured by the Muslim Ottoman empire, Nicholas seeks to promote a peaceful understanding between the religious traditions of his time. The dialogue not only includes Jews, Muslims, Roman Catholic, and Orthodox Christians, but also, among others, Indians and Bohemians. The latter were followers of the Czech proto-reformer Jan Hus and had upset the unity of Christendom in the West. While never doubting the truth of the Trinity, Nicholas argues that while there may indeed be many differences in practice and rituals, in principle, there is only one religion. In other words, God, being the coincidence of opposites, is also the principle that unites different traditions of faith. This does not make the truth of Christianity relative, but Christian theology already carries its own tools to formulate an inclusive vision of faith and religious practice, so to speak.

The Demise and Persistence of Negative Theology

Nicholas of Cusa's thinking on unity in diversity stands out as anticipating crucial themes of modernity. This, it could be argued, is also true for his understanding of science as a perpetual search for truth. As argued, negative theology plays a central role here too, suggesting that theology can play a formative and guiding part in the formulation of open-minded and critical thought. Even if the notorious description of the Middle Ages as the "Dark Ages" is to some degree meaningful—at least when considering negative theology's preoccupation with the "darkness of God"—negative theology in this way anticipates features of so-called Enlightenment philosophy in the seventeenth and eighteenth centuries. The crucial distinction is, of course, that while traditional negative theology derived its views of the world and human beings from its peculiar understanding of God, Enlightenment philosophy would in many cases reject the need for theological concepts altogether.

While being characteristic of medieval philosophy, Neoplatonic forms of negative theology did not disappear at the end of the Middle Ages. In the Italian Renaissance classical Platonism and Neoplatonism enjoyed a renewed interest with, for example, Marcilio Ficino (1433–99), who translated and commented on Dionysius's *Mystical Theology* and *The Divine Names*. Themes from medieval mysticism reappeared with Spanish Carmelites such as Teresa of Ávila (1515–82) and John of the Cross (1542–91), for whom negative theology also played a significant spiritual role. This is not least clear from the title of John's famous work *The Dark Night of The Soul* in which classical Dionysian themes receive a poetic form. For John, however, this was not so much a matter of apophatic logic, as it was a matter of experiencing a deep spiritual darkness, or even depression as some scholars have argued, as a prerequisite for union with God.[52]

As a result of a growing separation of faith and reason in both philosophy and theology, negative theology had increasingly become a matter of mystical spirituality, while its role in intellectual philosophy and metaphysics became less significant. Eckhartian themes continued to pop up outside the narrow confines of philosophy, however. For instance, in the influential works of the lay-theologian Jacob Böhme (1575–1624) and the poems of Silesius Angelus (1624–77). While this may suggest that negative theology in modernity was relegated from philosophy to the ranks of mysticism and poetry, it was not because theological reasoning disappeared from philosophy overnight. In the seventeenth century, French rationalist philosopher René Descartes (1596–1650) could argue, in somewhat similar fashion to Anselm before him, that the very possibility of having an idea of something divine, infinite, and incomprehensible suggests that God must exist. For Descartes, however, God's infinity was not qualitatively different

52. See Turner, *Darkness of God*, 227–44.

from finite things. It is simply the negation of finitude.[53] There is an element of negative theology in this claim, but it does not rest on the concept drawn on by earlier negative theologies, of God as the ineffable source of being in which everything participates. Another philosopher, Blaise Pascal (1623–62) and his sister Jacqueline Pascal (1625–61), a nun, could also talk about God's ineffability, but their reasoning rested more on a revival of Augustinian theology in contemporary Jansenism with its belief in an inscrutable predestination, than on Neoplatonic and Dionysian negative theology. With Immanuel Kant's famous critique of traditional metaphysics, theology was relegated to the department of morality and personal piety, leaving little room for traditional negative theology in philosophy.

The reason for the growing division between reason and faith in early modernity just hinted at—a division that also left its marks on how negative theology was approached and applied—resulted to a great extent from a rejection of the metaphysics of classical theology. Already in late medieval theology and philosophy, some rather different strains of thought had laid the foundations of the modern worldview.[54] Between the Middle Ages and modernity a new outlook arose concerning the relationship between God and creation, and between faith and knowledge, a development that was to alter the course of intellectual history, including negative theology. This novel outlook and the subsequent development in negative theology is the theme of the next chapter.

---

53. See Hart, *The Hidden and the Manifest*, 30.
54. See Blumenberg, *The Legitimacy of the Modern Age*.

III

New Negative Theologies

In darkness will be known the light.

—Jacob Böhme (1575–1624)

In this chapter we will take a few steps backwards in time in order to trace the origins of new forms of negative theology that developed in the modern era. With the development of nominalism and theological voluntarism in the fourteenth century, traditional metaphysics was gradually replaced by a sharper distinction between faith and knowledge. This distinction is deepened by the Reformation in the sixteenth century. The theology of Protestant reformer Martin Luther turns traditional negative theology upside down. It no longer concerns the *via negativa* from human beings to God, but God's negative way to human beings through the cross. With Jacob Böhme in the seventeenth century, this approach is reforged with themes from medieval mystical theology, leading to an emphasis on how the otherwise ineffable God is revealed through opposites in creation. Such dialectics would provide the impetus to the German idealist philosophy of G. W. F. Hegel and F. W. J. Schelling. Søren Kierkegaard may also be said to have reforged themes from negative theology in his response to rationalistic philosophy. In these forms negative theology would also leave its marks on the so-called dialectical theology of theologians like Karl Barth working in the interwar period. In the twentieth century, with philosophers like Franz Rosenzweig, Walter Benjamin, Emmanuel Levinas, and Jacques Derrida, the tradition became increasingly disconnected from its origins in traditional metaphysics. In recent years, however, negative theology has gained a renewed interest among theologians in response to postmodernity and deconstruction.

Ockham's Razor: Duns Scotus and William of Ockham

While negative theology continued to play a role in scholastic philosophy and medieval mysticism in the fourteenth and fifteenth centuries, Franciscan theologians John Duns Scotus and William of Ockham had already laid the foundations for a different approach to theology that had little need for the themes pertaining to traditional negative theology. The Scottish philosopher and theologian John Duns Scotus (1266–1308)—not to be confused with John Scotus Eriugena—is, perhaps, best known for his idea of the univocity of being. According to Scotus, the word "being" has exactly the same meaning when applied to God as when applied to created things. Whereas Thomas Aquinas had claimed, along with Dionysius, that words such as "good" and "being" do not have precisely the same meaning when applied to the creator as when applied to creatures, Duns Scotus held that the difference is above all a matter of *degree*. God has being, God is good, and so on, in the *same sense* as created beings, although to an *infinitely greater degree*. However, this also meant that God does not need to be defined through negations, as was the case in traditional negative theology.

In his own words, Duns Scotus had "no great love of negations." Negations only have value insofar as they support affirmations. For every negative definition of God, there must be a positive one. What we know only by negations is no more God than a chimera or nothing at all, says Duns Scotus.[1] Moreover, there is no real point in distinguishing between knowing what God's essence is and knowing that God exists, since we cannot know anything to exist without at least having some concept of it. This seriously challenges a fundamental idea in classical Christian negative theologies. For example, Irenaeus and Gregory of Nazianzus made it clear that knowing that God exists is one thing, while it is a very different thing to know what God essentially is. While God could be known indirectly through his works, according to traditional negative theology, knowing God in essence was impossible for human beings. For Duns Scotus, however, we cannot know that God exists without also knowing something about God. He thus rejects a central tenet of negative theology.

Like Scotus, the English philosopher and theologian William of Ockham (1285–1347) embraced the univocity of being, which effectively put God on the same plane of reality as all other beings. God is now one thing among other things, albeit eternal and infinite. Ockham further rejected the traditional Platonic idea of participation. Where Christian Platonists had maintained that creatures receive their being and goodness by participating in God's being and goodness, Ockham saw these concepts as hardly more than concepts. The only entities that really exist are individuals. Words such as "being" and "goodness" are names that exist only as mental concepts and not as universal ontological realities in which things can participate. This view is known as nominalism. Ockham is famous for his "nominalism" and it is closely related to the principle commonly known as Ockham's razor. According to this principle, we should not postulate unnecessary metaphysical entities in attempting to explain the world, but rather trim away superfluous speculation. Ockham's razor, not surprisingly, would also shave off many of the ideas relating to traditional negative theology, not least in its Neoplatonic forms. If only individual things have reality, then things cannot have their being by participation in God. In a sense, the distance between God and created beings has become even greater now. Why? Because as God is seen to

1. Duns Scotus, *On Natural Knowledge of God.*

be one thing on the same plane of existence as created things the infinite God becomes infinitely distant from creation rather than infinitely intimate to them. In classical negative theology, such as that developed by Clement of Alexandria, Gregory of Nyssa, and Neoplatonic philosophy, while God was radically different from the world, everything had its being by participating in God. As such, God was seen to be *infinitely close*, while being incomprehensible and ineffable because of the infinity and simplicity of the divine nature. Negating our notions of God was seen to be a way of relating in silence to the God who is radically different, but infinitely close. However, if God is no longer "being itself" in which individual beings participate, but rather one being (albeit the supreme being) among others, as implied by nominalism, this also means that negative theology can hardly be a way to union with God.

A residue of negative theology might, however, be found in the voluntaristic depiction of God shared to some degree by Duns Scotus and Ockham. As a theological position, voluntarism maintains that God is primarily defined by his power or will (*voluntas*). While Thomas Aquinas had seen "goodness" as a property of God in which created beings can participate, Duns Scotus and Ockham argued that what we call good is simply what God wills. In other words, God does not will something because it is good; rather, it is God's willing something that *makes* it good. This also meant, however, that there are no limits to what God can will, the only exception being violations of the principle of non-contradiction. God is ruled by his own will alone. From this arises a distinction between God's ordained will or power, which we can know, and God's absolute will or power, which is as inconceivable as it is unpredictable. In Ockham's philosophy in particular, the infinite God is so removed from creation that there is really nothing to connect the two except for his inscrutable will. Such voluntarism elevates the divine will and severs it from God's goodness in a way that classical theology did not. In classical theology, God's will was seen as an expression of his goodness, but in voluntaristic theology, God's goodness is defined by God's will alone. However, if

God is *absolutely* free, dependent on his own will and sovereign power alone, then God must surely be incomprehensible to human reason. In this way, the voluntaristic philosophy of Scotus and Ockham takes over some of the basic concerns that first forged negative theology, while leaving behind the framework in which it had traditionally been formulated. Nominalism and voluntarism preserve something of negative theology, but in a *warped* way, so to speak.

Furthermore, Ockham argued that the doctrine of the Trinity is contradictory in its claims that God is both one and three. This does not mean it should be rejected, but it cannot be a matter of knowledge, only of faith. In this way, Ockham's views led to a new and sharper distinction between faith and reason, theology and philosophy. While this hardly amounts to negative theology in the classical sense, Ockham's approach to faith led to a fideism that can sometimes, at a superficial level, look like a negative theology. Perhaps we can even argue that voluntarism and nominalism had become the starting points for a new kind of negative theology in the modern age. At least this seems to be the case as we approach the time of the Reformation.

The Hidden God: Martin Luther and the Reformation

The Protestant Reformation in the sixteenth century is typically associated with names such as Martin Luther (1483–1546) and Huldrich Zwingli (1484–1531), and their emphasis on Scripture as the sole authority of faith. In regards to theology and philosophy, this resulted in the rejection of large parts of medieval scholastic philosophy. Things were, however, more complex as strains of medieval philosophy and theology continued to play a role. Luther had studied nominalist philosophy and in one of his table talks allegedly declared himself to belong to "Ockham's party."[2] This is not to say, however, that Luther was completely hostile to mysticism and negative theology in the Neoplatonic tradition.

2. Luther, *Table Talk* WA 6, 195.

New Negative Theologies

Early on, Luther published an edition of *Theologia Deutsch*, a short treatise by an unknown author who was most likely influenced by medieval mystics like Meister Eckhart and Johannes Tauler. The idea that we must go through a negative experience of spiritual death in order to reach salvation proved inspirational for Luther, who would also talk of faith and salvation in terms of *resignatio ad infernum*, that is, yielding to the experience of a spiritual hell as a prerequisite for accepting God's inscrutable will, whatever it might be. Luther, however, later came to reconsider these issues. This may have been due to what he perceived to be an abuse of mystical theology by some of his contemporaries, such as the Anabaptists and the self-pronounced prophet Thomas Müntzer associated with the peasant revolt in 1525. Inspired by texts like the *Theologia Deutsch*, these radical reformers had taken a mystic approach similar to that of Meister Eckhart, even to the degree of arguing that human beings must be united to God's "nothing" by themselves becoming "nothing."

This was the case for the Anabaptist leader Hans Denck (c. 1500–1527), and the so-called godless painters, Sebald Beham and his brother Barthel, who had allegedly claimed that God "is not." While this led to an accusation of atheism by the Lutheran authorities in Nuremberg, for Hans Denck the idea was mystical in that God was "nothing" by virtue of being quite opposite to human nature as long as human nature is "something." Conversely, only by becoming "nothing," says Denck, can a person be united to God's incomprehensible "nothing." This "nothing" is in fact the highest "something."[3] Such union to God happens when the human soul gives itself up to God's spirit in yieldedness or *Gelassenheit* by ceasing all activities. For Anabaptists with spiritualist leanings, this experience of becoming nothing should precede baptism. The staunch commitment to believers' baptism separated the Anabaptists from the magisterial reformers, Luther and Zwingli. While many Anabaptists were pacifists, the religious and political fanaticism that sometimes came to characterize the Radical Reformation

3. Denck, *Schriften* 2.33, 15–24.

was also among the reasons why Luther would eventually reject this kind of mysticism.

Luther, in some of his early lectures on the Psalms, had applied the traditional reading to the story of Moses as a narrative about God's incomprehensibility. When, on the one hand, Psalm 18 declares that God has made darkness his hiding place and, on the other, the First Epistle to Timothy says that God hides in an unapproachable light, Luther argues that this means that God is beyond both darkness and light.[4] So far, Luther agrees with the Neoplatonic and Dionysian tradition in Christian theology. Luther, however, increasingly takes leave of the traditional forms of negative theology as he emphasizes that salvation is only found in the preached Word of God, not in speculative theology, mysticism, or inward revelation. In his *Heidelberg Disputation* from 1518, Luther argues that there is no way of knowing God, except when he hides under the form of his opposite. God is only known through suffering, and his glory is revealed through the poverty of the cross. For this reason, Luther argues, a true theologian does not become wise through natural theology and philosophical speculation, but only through the contradiction of the cross.

Luther's rejection of theological speculation pertains to what is sometimes called a "destruction of metaphysics," but this does not mean that Luther had no need at all for negative theology. Rather, through his destruction of metaphysics, Luther turned the *via negativa* upside down.[5] Negations are now not a way for human beings to reach the ineffable God, but God's way of reaching human beings by negating himself in the incarnation and the cross. When God tells Moses that he cannot see God's face, this, for Luther, expresses the fact that no one can reach God except through God's revelation in Christ.

Luther's inversion of negative theology corresponds to his Augustinian emphasis on the need for grace, which was arguably also a reason for Luther to prefer infant baptism over believers'

---

4. Luther, *On the Psalms* WA 3, 124.

5. See Moltmann, *The Crucified God*, 299–309. See also Mjaaland, *The Hidden God.*

baptism. Human beings are incapable of choosing God. Salvation depends on God choosing us. Luther formulated this position over against the Dutch humanist scholar Erasmus of Rotterdam (1469–1536). In a defense of human free will, the latter had argued that God wills the salvation of all humanity, but that human beings are free to reject God's salvation. For Erasmus, this meant that evil and damnation must be the result of human abuse of free will. Luther disagreed and argued in his *On the Bondage of the Will* from 1525 that while God does not, according to his revealed word, wish for the death of the sinner, there is more to say since, outside the revelation of his word, God is still hidden. As "the hidden God" (*deus absconditus*), God has predestined the majority of human beings to damnation, having decided prior to the act of creation who will believe and who will not.[6] In other words, there is no such thing as human free will since everything has been decided beforehand by the hidden God. Luther argues that while Satan and God appear to be enemies fighting over the human soul, in fact, Satan is a tool of the hidden God.[7] While God, as revealed in his word, declared himself to be good, God as hidden outside his word is also the cause of evil and suffering. This is why Luther can argue that the highest degree of faith is to call God good and righteous even while accepting that God has created the vast majority of humankind with the sole purpose of damnation.

Luther thereby affirms important aspects of the voluntaristic understanding of God as a pure, sovereign will, beyond human comprehension. The good is not defined by abstract categories, but by God's will, even if it seems to contradict everything that we intuitively call "good." For Luther, the belief in God's absolute power was required in order to trust that everything is in the hands of God.[8] The reality of the hidden God must be affirmed to make it clear that God is in control. The aim is not to speculate about the nature of God outside revelation, but, on the contrary, that we may be led to take refuge in the revealed word of God. While

6. Luther, *On the Bondage of the Will* WA 18, 636.

7. Luther, *On the Bondage of the Will* WA 18, 709.

8. Luther, *On the Bondage of the Will* WA 18, 619.

Luther's claims about the hidden God may sound preposterous, the purpose is arguably not to formulate a speculative doctrine about what God is outside of his revelation. If this side of Luther's theology may be called negative theology, its primary purpose is to affirm the positive theology pertaining to the proclamation of salvation by faith alone. In this way, negative theology becomes the dark backdrop for the gospel, so to speak. If Luther's notion of the hidden God can be described as a kind of negative theology, it should be equally clear that we are dealing with a negative theology of very a different kind from that known by the earlier Christian tradition.

The more mystical forms of negative theology were to some degree kept alive by spiritualist theologians after the reformation, due to the influence of Hans Denck and others. It was, however, Luther's theological perspective that became dominant in mainline Protestantism. Luther's Augustinian beliefs about predestination and the lack of a human free will were affirmed by the reformed, Calvinist doctrines of a double predestination, while also being echoed on Roman Catholic ground in later Jansenist theology. This theology equally emphasized predestination and the inability of human beings to understand God's reasons. As mentioned in the first part above, Blaise Pascal and his sister Jacqueline, like Luther, wrote about the hidden nature of God and the fact that God can only be known indirectly through suffering.[9]

In both Catholic and Lutheran contexts the notion of the hidden God and its correlating beliefs in a double predestination met opposition as, for example, the king of Denmark forbade the new Lutheran pastors to discuss the subject in their sermons. Parts of Lutheran theology would, however, develop in a somewhat different direction, not least as a new and more speculative kind of negative theology appeared with radical pietists and theosophists. Notable among these new negative theologians was Jacob Böhme. We will now turn our attention to this current of negative theology in the post-Reformation period.

9. See Conley, *The Other Pascals.*

The Groundlessness of God: Jacob Böhme

New perspectives on negative theology saw the light of day with Jacob Böhme (1575–1624). His writings became hugely influential from the seventeenth century onwards, not least in continental radical pietism, but also in an English context with the Quakers and Philadelphians (although in less apophatic forms). A shoemaker by trade, Böhme has often been described as an original and self-taught thinker. His thinking does, however, bear clear traces of the influence of Reformation spiritualists and alchemists, such as Paracelsus and Caspar Schwenckfeld. Böhme himself described how since his youth he had received a number of revelations leading him to certain insights into the nature of God and the universe. Parts of Böhme's later works contain elements akin to traditional negative theology, and at times even the more radical kinds of negative theology associated with much earlier theologians like Basilides and Meister Eckhart.

In his book *On the Election of Grace*, Böhme took issue with the idea prevalent in Protestant theology at the time that God contains two wills—one evil and one good. While this idea reflects Luther's belief in the hidden God who is the source of evil and suffering in the world, Böhme rejects this notion as being at odds with the unity and oneness of God. God as the "eternal One" is neither darkness nor light, and neither love nor anger.[10] Böhme argues that we cannot say that God is "this or that evil or good, which has distinction in itself," for God is without or beyond nature and creature. While God is "the only being," God is simultaneously "the Nothing and the All-things." Böhme even describes God as an "eternal Nothing" and an "Abyss" without will. Not surprisingly, God as such is also described in terms familiar to negative theology as an "incomprehensible Nothing."

God is not just an abyss, however. He is also famously named by Böhme as the *Ungrund* or unground. That God can be called the *Ungrund* has to do with God's eternal freedom, which is not grounded in anything. As argued later by the Russian

10. Böhme, *On the Election of Grace* 1, 3–7.

proto-existentialist philosopher Nicolai Berdyaev, Böhme's philosophy was, first of all, a matter of the *"mē*-ontological" freedom that human beings share with God. This freedom is based in *non-being*, the *mē on* that is beyond being.[11] Precisely since God is eternal freedom, God cannot be reduced to any finite thing, which is why God's *Ungrund* can also be described as "darkness" and "nothing."

It may perhaps be argued that in this way, in Böhme, the voluntarism inherited from Duns Scotus and Ockham through Luther turns out to imply a metaphysical belief about the nothingness of God as somehow preceding being. Being presupposes nothing, in other words. This nothing, which is the *Ungrund*, longs to be something, says Böhme. This is how something comes about in the first place. In Böhme's view, the Trinity is God's self-realization. Although the abyss of God is without will, it nevertheless generates in itself a comprehensible will. The abyss can thus be described as Father, while the generated, second will, can be described as Son. In this second will, the nothing finds itself as something, says Böhme, while describing the Spirit as the being and life of the Father and the Son.

Although he is eternal freedom, God longs to be revealed in creation. This is where the election of good and evil comes into the picture. According to Böhme, the election for good and evil is only a reality in creation, and not in God as such. In creation, everything interrelates through contrasts. God is good, not evil, but God is revealed when overcoming evil with good. In this way, even the fall seems to have been a necessary step in God's self-revelation as good. If there was no opposition, the hidden God would have stayed hidden, says Böhme.[12] It seems that this is why there must be in creation both an election of evil and good. There is both a fire of love and a fire of wrath that come from God, as Böhme puts it. Although both come from the same principle, they are divided in order that the one may be revealed in the other: "In the darkness will be known the light," says Böhme, "otherwise nothing would

11. Berdyaev, "Studies Concerning Jacob Boehme," 34–62.

12. Böhme, *The Way to Christ* 1, 9.

be revealed." Revelation is, in other words, negatively dependent on hiddenness.

Even if Böhme's ideas are decidedly more speculative than Luther's notions of the hidden God, there are clear similarities. Like Luther's hidden God, for Böhme, the *Ungrund* is the dark backdrop that makes it necessary for God to reveal himself through opposites. While clearly affirming certain themes in traditional negative theology, Böhme and Luther agree, however, that darkness and incomprehensibility are not the final aim or destination, but only the beginning of a spiritual journey directed at the positive self-manifestation of God. Salvation does not consist in the return to the *Ungrund*, nothing, and darkness, but in becoming a person that relates to God as revealed in Christ. Arguably, this is why in spite of similarities to gnostic speculations, Böhme's theosophy would nevertheless turn out to be largely compatible with an orthodox emphasis on the need for faith in Christ. It would, however, also become the impetus for new developments in philosophy and theology in the nineteenth century.

The *Ungrund* Revisited: German Idealism and Søren Kierkegaard

In the eighteenth century, a less speculative and more rationalistic approach to theology had become mainstream with Enlightenment philosophy. Immanuel Kant famously argued that philosophical claims about God will always lead to contradictions or antinomies. While this may seem similar to the claim of classical negative theology that God is beyond opposites, the point for Kant was more in line with the nominalism of Ockham: if metaphysics leads to logical contradictions, this only shows that there are limits to how far metaphysics can take us. Whatever we say about God is a matter of faith rather than reason. The theosophical speculations of Jacob Böhme became useful again, however, in German idealism in the nineteenth century.

The idea that God makes himself known by working through opposites in creation proved useful not least for G. W. F. Hegel

(1770–1831), who described Böhme as the "teutonic" (that is, German) philosopher. In Hegel's dialectical philosophy, all concepts are made up of pairs of contraries. For example, "temperature" is made up of "hot" and "cold." In his *Science of Logic,* Hegel described how "becoming" contains the contraries "being" and "nothing." Pure being, says Hegel, is indeterminate. It is nothing in particular and, as such, it is "nothing." However, in becoming, being and nothing vanish in their opposition. Every concept must be defined dialectically in this way through its opposite. When we move from negation to the negation of negation, we do not, however, end up with silence or "unknowing," as in traditional negative theologies, but with a fully rational system that contains all opposites. While negation plays a crucial role in Hegel's thinking, the aim is not a mystical unknowing, but *absolute knowing.* Hegel could, for this reason, even argue that the ineffable is nothing else than the untrue or the irrational.[13]

Hegel's thinking led to what many perceived as a problematic understanding of the relationship between God and the world. The absolute is the identity of the identical and the non-identical, as Hegel puts it. This also means, however, that the traditional distinction between God and the world is overcome in the absolute. God, it seems, is more or less identical to the world, making the traditional notions of God superfluous. Such pantheism also seems to denigrate human freedom, since everything must be determined by the dialectics of world history where the absolute finds self-recognition. F. H. Jacobi (1743–1819), Hegel's contemporary, had already coined the term "nihilism" as a critique of the pantheistic philosophy associated with Baruch Spinoza (1632–1677) that made the world and God identical in such a way as to apparently exclude human freedom and responsibility. If God is identical to the world in such a way that the course of the world is absolutely determined by God, it seems there can be no human freedom. To avoid the pantheism and determinism that were similarly seen to follow on from Hegel's system, philosophers and theologians like Friedrich Schelling and Søren Kierkegaard argued that God

13. Hegel, *The Phenomenology of Spirit,* 66.

must be distinct from the world, and that he must, to some degree, transcend philosophical systems. Human freedom must be understood as irreducible to objective facts. In this context, elements of negative theology reemerge and take new forms.

In his lectures on human freedom, Friedrich Schelling (1775–1854) argued that while it is true that nothing can exist outside of God, if we are to avoid pantheism, then everything must be grounded in something within God that is different from God. This is where Böhme's idea of God's *Ungrund* once again becomes useful. Human freedom is derived from the freedom of the *Ungrund*, which is never exhausted in being but continues to be the dark backdrop of being, so to speak.[14] All birth is birth from darkness into light, says Schelling. The *Ungrund* is an absolute indifference preceding all opposites. It splits into two beginnings in being, but only so that the two can be made one again. Reminiscent of earlier Protestant thought, in his *Ages of the World*, Schelling explains how God's freedom lies in a tension between two opposite wills, a "no" and a "yes." These oppose and seek revelation respectively, which is why God can only be revealed through opposites. "No" precedes "yes," wrath precedes love. Importantly, God does not change from being hidden to being revealed, but continues to be the hidden God in spite of being revealed.[15]

As with Luther, the hidden God continues to be the negative backdrop for God's positive revelation. This also means that the foundation of philosophy is something unthinkable that precedes thinking, something that grounds reason, while being itself irrational. Schelling, however, rejects the idea associated with traditional negative theologies where God is said to be metaphorically above or beyond being. Rather, God must be conceived as *prior to* being, like the dark ground from which being emerges. This is one of the reasons why Schelling's philosophy has been interpreted as a radical materialism, basically claiming that reason and spirit are

14. Schelling, *Philosophical Investigations into the Essence of Human Freedom*, 68.

15. Schelling, *The Ages of the World*, 144.

the product of irrational matter.[16] Again, however, the main point is that we do not move from light into the darkness of unknowing as in some medieval negative theologies. On the contrary, we move from darkness into light, from the hidden to the revealed God that nevertheless stays hidden.

Somewhat similar to Schelling, but against the rationalism of Hegel, the Danish philosopher Søren Kierkegaard emphasized human freedom from a theological perspective where God is only revealed indirectly through paradoxes. Human existence cannot be reduced to objective facts. Faith appears when human reason is destroyed by its encounter with the paradoxes of the absolute. God cannot be the object of knowledge, but only a matter of a faith that transcends knowledge. Kierkegaard develops this line of thought in his *Concluding Unscientific Postscript to Philosophical Fragments*. Like Schelling, he denied the possibility of a negative way to God as that associated with traditional negative theology. This was because there can be no objectivity in God, but only subjectivity. God is not this or that thing, which means God cannot be the object of any intellectual method. Not unlike Meister Eckhart, for this reason Kierkegaard can also talk of God as somehow "nothing." In a note in his journals, he makes the peculiar claim that "nothing" is, in fact, better than "something." When it comes to relative, finite things, it is true that "something" is better than "nothing," but when it comes to the infinite and absolute, "nothing" is better than "something."[17]

Again, this explains why God, according to Kierkegaard, cannot be made an object of thought, but only be known indirectly through paradoxes. There is a "qualitative difference" between God and human beings that makes God inaccessible to human reason. Faith can be described as a "passion for the uncertain," which is also why God cannot be contained in any kind of philosophical or theological system. Every attempt at institutionalizing the Christian faith must be resisted, as Kierkegaard himself increasingly

16. See Slavoj Žižek's preface to Schelling, *The Ages of the World*.

17. Kierkegaard, *Journals* NB28. See also Kline, *Passion for Nothing*, and Law, *Kierkegaard as Negative Theologian*.

did, engaging in a one-man battle against academic theology and the Lutheran state church and its representatives. The faith of the individual transcends any attempt at merging absolute truth with the common culture and moral values of Christendom.

When Kierkegaard in his pseudonymous work *Fear and Trembling* described Abraham's faith as morally unintelligible, there is arguably also an element of negative theology present. When God requires that Abraham kill his son Isaac as an offer to God, Abraham is thereby separated from everything common to human moral rationality. This is why Abraham's faith cannot be comprehended but only be described in terms of silence. In this way, the metaphysical individualism originally associated with nominalism and theological voluntarism arguably crops up again as a kind of religious individualism that equally emphasizes the inscrutability of God's will. God cannot, for Kierkegaard, be an objective fact in a rational system, but can only be approached through the faith and passion of the believing subject. As such, a form of negative theology is expressed in a radical pietism that leads to a strong emphasis on individual faith over against objective religion and cultural Christianity.

The "Yes" in Our "No": The Death of God, Dialectical Theology and Karl Barth

In spite of cultural critics like Søren Kierkegaard, the nineteenth century was to a large degree characterized by an optimistic understanding of humanity and God. A non-dogmatic approach to theological doctrines and a faith in cultural progress was the hallmark of what has often been called liberal theology. It seemed, however, that with cultural and scientific progress, God became increasingly irrelevant for modern society. The "death of God" diagnosed by the German philosopher Friedrich Nietzsche (1844–1900) as characteristic of the modern, secular age made it necessary for theologians to reconsider how theology can nevertheless talk of God. This need only became more urgent as the liberal faith in progress and "cultural Christianity" was shattered by the horrors of the First World War. Emerging from the empty foxholes of war-ridden continental Europe came a bleaker and more pessimistic view of human nature, religion, and theology.

A typical response to the experience of the death of God was, in post-war theology, that God is present exactly in his absence. This was argued by, for example, the French-Jewish philosopher Simone Weil (1909–43), for whom this was the reason why we must pass through a purifying atheism in order to reach God. Insofar as religion is a source of consolation, it is a hindrance to true faith, says Weil. In this, atheism can be a kind of purification that negates the false God that prevents us from coming into contact with the true God. There is no "God" in the sense of something that can be conceived, but this is why we need to be purified of whatever we conceive of as God.[18] As the Danish Lutheran pastor-theologian Johannes Horstmann (1915–2015) would later put it, although writing from a very different perspective, the "death of God" is the experience in which God is present with those who can no longer sing his praises.[19] In the modern, secular age, God is experienced as a lack, as something absent, but this is exactly the experience that enables faith today. Moreover, the "death of God" may even be the product of Christianity itself as it produces the nihilism and atheism that are the preconditions of true Christian faith purified of false notions about God.

Pivotal to the formulation of such theology in the period after the First World War, was the Swiss pastor and reformed theologian Karl Barth (1886–1968), whose *The Epistle to the Romans* became the epitome of so-called dialectical theology. Dialectical theology emphasized the "qualitative difference" between God and humanity, which Kierkegaard had talked about, while also incorporating elements akin to the Böhmist idea that God's revelation always proceeds through contradictions. Against the bankrupt religious and cultural optimism of liberal theology, Karl Barth described "religion" as humanity's vain attempt at reaching God by its own means. Revelation is, on the contrary, like a grenade that splits

18. Weil, *Gravity and Grace*, 103.

19. Horstmann, "Kristendom og existens."

everything within its blast radius into pieces. God reveals himself as the negation of all our ideas about who and what God is. The true God is the negation of the "non-god" of this world. There can be no way from humanity to God, not even a negative way, argues Barth, thereby closing the door for any kind of traditional negative theology. However, as God is revealed as the negation of all human ideals and ideologies, God must, nevertheless, be described in the negative in order not to be made into an idea controllable by human rationality. God, says Barth, is the "yes" in our "no," and the "no" in our "yes," while truth is beyond every negation and affirmation.[20] This sounds a lot like traditional negative theology.

In his early sermons, Barth was preoccupied with the ineffability of revelation. A good example is one of the sermons co-authored with his colleague Eduard Thurneysen. Drawing on an image from the Chinese philosopher Lao-Tse, this sermon compares our thoughts to the spokes in a wagon wheel that must converge in an empty hole if the wheel is to fit around its axle. In the same way, our theological thoughts must be open to what lies beyond mere concepts of God. The death and resurrection of Christ show us that our entire theological language only has value as witness to an incomprehensible divine reality that breaks into the world from beyond.[21] Another sermon more dramatically recalls how a troupe of players had recently produced the "dance of death" in the town.[22] Being gathered around death, we are reminded that death is the one central point of the world. Only behind this central point of death does a new, central point arise with the resurrection. While death and resurrection are, of course, core elements in traditional Christian preaching, the inevitable need for negation again displays similarities with negative theology. The way to life goes through a total negation of everything human. To this degree, Barth and Thurneysen agreed with Nietzsche that the human is "something that must be overcome." This overcoming, however, happens not by the creation of the "superman" but through the

20. Barth, *Romans*, 185.

21. Barth and Thurneysen, *Come Holy Spirit*, 158–70.

22. Barth and Thurneysen, *Come Holy Spirit*, 176–77.

death and resurrection of humanity with Christ.[23] This death is, to a large degree, also a matter of dying to our mistaken conceptions about God. Our death with Christ is also the death of our religious idols and the no-god of this world. As such, dialectical theology does contain an apophatic element in its "unsaying" of our religious notions of God.

It may even seem that much of this resembles, for example, Meister Eckhart's prayer to be freed of "God." As with earlier negative theologies, we only arrive at a true notion of God as unknown by way of the negation of our misconceptions of the God that we think we know. Dialectical theology, however, does not so much conceive of a union with God as a result of this negation, but rather seeks to establish humanity as a finite being freed from mistaken idealism and as such fit for life in the secular age. It should not be overlooked that there was a political import to the negation of idealism, even if dialectical theologians in the interwar period disagreed on the exact practical consequences of the critique of moral idealism. Some joined hands with the Marxist critique of bourgeois idealism, while others were more conservative in their defense of traditional values. In both cases, the negation of human ideals, religiosity, and aspirations led to a re-evaluation of theology.

Barth gradually developed a much more positive and Christocentric perspective on theology, arguing in his *Church Dogmatics* and elsewhere that the revelation in Christ puts an end to all religious mysticism. The Lutheran idea of a "hidden god" responsible for evil and destruction in the world was even a factor in the embrace of National Socialism by the German Christians, Barth argued. This was in itself enough of a reason for focusing solely on the revealed God in Christ instead of speculating about God's hidden will. The preoccupation with ineffability and negation would live on in different forms, however, especially in twentieth-century philosophy.

---

23. Barth and Thurneysen, *Come Holy Spirit*, 123.

Against Totality: Franz Rosenzweig and Emmanuel Levinas

The First World War did not just result in reorientation in Christian theology, but would also become a catalyst for new philosophical tendencies in post-war Jewish thought.[24] In 1921, the same year as the second edition of Karl Barth's *The Epistle to the Romans* was published, came Franz Rosenzweig's *The Star of Redemption*, a book that Rosenzweig began working on while at the front in the Balkans. Franz Rosenzweig (1886–1929), having first identified as a Hegelian, had become critical of Hegel's idea of history as the unfolding of a rational, coherent whole, and turned instead to Schelling's philosophy, described above. Death, and the experience of the fear of death, reveals the irreducible particularity of each human person. Philosophy's attempt at reducing every particular thing to a single, absolute origin must, then, be resisted. God, the world, and the human self are rooted in their own particularity. In themselves, God, the world, and the self are nothing. They are, however, their own nothing, so to speak. Only through creation, revelation, and redemption do the three become something in mutual relation to each other.

While Rosenzweig's thinking was critical of negative theology as well as of Barth's dialectical theology, it begins in a rather apophatic attitude to theology: "Of God we know nothing," writes Rosenzweig.[25] However, this ignorance, he adds, is precisely an "ignorance of God." As such our ignorance of God is the beginning of our knowledge of God. In this way Rosenzweig rejects what he conceives to be the basic idea of traditional negative theology that seeks to abolish all assertions about God's attributes. Such theology leads from "something" to "nothing" and will finally end up where mysticism and atheism shake hands. Instead, Rosenzweig recommends taking the path from "nothing" to "something." This is, in fact, how history itself moves towards redemption. This does not mean that we simply begin with nothing and end up in being,

---

24. See Fagenblat, *Negative Theology as Jewish Modernity*.

25. Rosenzweig, *The Star of Redemption*, 23–33.

as a simplistic reading of, for example, Böhme and Hegel might suggest. History not only originates in an incomprehensible nothing, but it also moves towards its fulfillment in the God who continues to be beyond comprehension. The process of redemption takes place in God's revealed name, writes Rosenzweig, but the end, he adds, is nameless. The end is above any name: "Beyond the word there shines silence." In this way, even if he rejects traditional negative theology, Rosenzweig ends up affirming key elements of apophatic thinking. We must anticipate the silence into which the name of God and we together will one day sink, says Rosenzweig.[26] This anticipation takes place in the religious practices of Judaism and Christianity. Liturgy and ethical practices are thus the only adequate outcome of theology.

A somewhat similar, although more revolutionary, attitude was displayed by Walter Benjamin (1892–1940), another Jewish philosopher of the interwar period. Benjamin, in his *Theologico-Political Fragment*, described the Messianic kingdom as breaking into history as a revolutionary contradiction of the status quo.[27] While human activity cannot directly contribute to furthering the Messianic kingdom, it can do so indirectly by creating the negative conditions that must be contradicted by the Messianic. In this way, Benjamin could even recommend a kind of "methodological nihilism" as a political equivalent to negative theology. As in dialectical theology the necessity of negations follows from the fact that the kingdom of God cannot be comprehended or made an object of thought. In this way Benjamin, like Rosenzweig, displayed a critical attitude to the totalizing tendencies of the Hegelian system while preserving some of its dialectical methodology. Only from the outside, only through revelation that breaks into the world, can the Messianic kingdom become present or redemption take place. Such criticism of totality would be influential in, for example, Theodor W. Adorno's "negative dialectics," which likewise emphasized

---

26. Rosenzweig, *The Star of Redemption*, 384.

27. Benjamin, "Theologico-Political Fragment."

the need for negations in order to avoid the totalizing tendencies of traditional philosophy.[28]

An approach bearing perhaps clearer resemblances to traditional negative theology would survive in the equally influential critique of "totality" appearing in the works of French-Lithuanian Jewish philosopher Emmanuel Levinas (1906–95). During the Second World War, Levinas had spent several years as a prisoner of war in a camp near Hannover. It should come as no surprise, then, that his philosophy was fundamentally anti-totalitarian. Inspired not least by Franz Rosenzweig, his philosophy can be read to a great extent as an attempt to formulate an alternative to traditional philosophy, since the latter had, in Levinas's view, failed to acknowledge the dignity of "the other" person. From its very inception, philosophy has been haunted by a fear of "the other that remains the other," argues Levinas, which is why philosophy has always attempted to subject everything to an all-encompassing ontology, a theory of "being."[29] Levinas catches glimpses of alternative conceptions, not least in the claim made by Socrates in Plato's *The Republic* that the good is beyond being. If the good is really *beyond* being, then philosophy cannot be a matter of painting a comprehensive picture of being, but must begin, instead, with the good itself rather than being. In other words, ethics, rather than ontology, must be conceived as "the first philosophy." While this is obviously a rather positive statement, there are clear similarities with those forms of traditional negative theology that placed the good somehow beyond or above being.

Levinas also drew critically on the influential German philosopher Martin Heidegger (1889–1976), who described traditional metaphysics critically as "onto-theology," understood as an attempt at deriving "what is" (*to on*) from theology. This derivation has been unsuccessful, Heidegger argued, since being differs from beings and cannot for this reason be reduced to a "highest being."

28. While Adorno's thought has been likened to negative theology, there is not much explicit "theology" in his negative dialectics. Finlayson, "Notes on Negative Theology and Adorno's Negative Dialectics."

29. Levinas, *Totality and Infinity*, 42.

So far so good, but what was missing in Heidegger's analysis, according to Levinas, was an ethical concern for "the other." Rather than trying to box up everything that exists inside a totality of being, philosophy should make us open to "the other" who cannot be contained in an ontological system. In the encounter with the other we experience the infinite that escapes our grasp. Echoing the long tradition of negative theology, Levinas uses the story of Moses, who is allowed to see God's back, but not his face.[30] In a similar fashion, the other person—that is, whatever human being that we meet—does not appear to us as a thing or an object among other objects. The other person transcends our categories of being. We cannot perceive the other directly, but the other is known through the "trace" they leave in the world. We know that we are dealing with the other when we perceive their trace in the face of other persons, but we cannot make the other a direct object of thought or language.

Even if Levinas denies that negation can ever take us outside "being" and make what is beyond being comprehensible to us, there are clear similarities with classical negative theology in his approach to the human person perceived as the other. For example, we can think of Gregory of Nyssa's insistence that we only have an indirect, negative definition of what it means to be a human made in the image of the ineffable God. However, in clear distinction from classical forms of negative theology, Levinas does not suggest that we can somehow "participate" in the other. In fact, participation is a denial of the divine, says Levinas in *Totality and Infinity*. This is because the idea of participation seeks to reduce the other to an object or a part of a totality.[31] The notion of participation, in other words, reduces "the other" to "the same." Such a reduction almost does violence to the other, says Levinas. In a way, Levinas thereby radicalizes elements from traditional negative theology.

While leaving little room for the traditional theological motif of participation, Levinas's thinking is thus an uncompromising defense of the "otherness" of the good and the other person against

30. Levinas, "Meaning and Sense," 75–107.

31. See Zimmermann, *Levinas and Theology*, 138.

all attempts at subsuming everything under a totalizing system. The rejection of participatory ontology may also be said, however, to exemplify how negative theology in its modern form is generally shaped by nominalism (as described above), rather than by classical negative theology. In nominalism, as formulated by William of Ockham, the only things that really exists are individuals, leaving little room for an idea of a shared humanity or human participation in God. As argued by some contemporary theologians, this rejection of classical participatory ontology is really what led to the nihilism that characterizes modern and postmodern philosophy and culture.[32]

Deconstruction: Jacques Derrida and Postmodern Theology

This part of our journey through negative theology began with a discussion of how voluntarism and nominalism reshaped the theological landscape in the late Middle Ages. This culminated in a reversal of negative theology in the theology of Martin Luther. Theology did not now consist in a negative way from us to God, but in God's way to us through the negation of the cross. Today theologians have noted how this "destruction" of metaphysics has continued all the way up to the present.[33] For example, Martin Heidegger's rejection of traditional philosophy as "onto-theology" was not entirely new, but must be seen as a continuation of the destruction of metaphysics already begun in the Reformation period.

In the latter part of the twentieth century, this destruction was continued as "deconstruction" in the influential works of the French philosopher Jacques Derrida (1930–2004), of Algerian-Jewish origin. Derrida was highly critical of what he called the "metaphysics of presence," a phenomenon that he found to be characteristic of most traditional metaphysics as well as the thinking of Heidegger. Traditional metaphysics had prioritized presence

---

32. See Milbank, *Theology and Social Theory*.

33. Mjaaland, *The Hidden God*.

over absence as the source of meaning. However, meaning can never be fully present. What we often perceive as clearly defined concepts and ideals are much more indeterminate than we are prone to think. This does not mean that there is no such things as meaning and truth, but as an approach to philosophy, deconstruction seeks to show that language is irreducibly complex in a way that makes meaning and even truth uncertain.

For Derrida, the instability of the relationship between language and meaning had to do with the fact that the meaning of words can only be defined in relation to differences, which must in turn be defined in relation to further differences, and so on. In order to express this fact, Derrida coined the term *différance*, referring to how the meaning of language is deferred endlessly through differences. To be more precise, *différance* is the origin or production of differences, but as such it is neither a word nor a concept.[34] While being aware of possible similarities, Derrida denied that his notion of *différance* implied a kind of negative theology. This is so, he argued, even if *différance* is not "something," but can only be defined by saying what it is not. Derrida admits that this approach shows obvious similarities with negative theologies, but *différance* should not, he says, be confused with a highest being or a being beyond being, as negative theologies have often defined God.

In a way, however, Derrida arguably does exactly what the more radical forms of negative theology had done before him, when they, for example, spoke of God as "nothing," not even "beyond being." Commentators have observed that, similar to how "being" depends on "nothing," according to Heidegger, meaning for Derrida depends on a nothing towards which language must continuously move, but can never reach. As theologian Conor Cunningham puts it, "*différance* is the trace of the Plotinian One, which is non-being."[35] Deconstruction may be said to contain an apophatic attitude to language, to the degree that whatever we conceive of as definite concepts must be unsaid in order to open

---

34. Derrida, "Différance." See also Derrida, "How to Avoid Speaking: Denials."

35. Cunningham, *Genealogy of Nihilism*, 155.

up to whatever more is beyond what we presently grasp. It has also been argued that deconstruction for this reason is a kind of nihilism, since meaning then presupposes nothing or meaninglessness. Rather than defending nihilism, however, Derrida emphasized that his thought was an attempt at doing philosophy based on the responsibility towards "the other," not unlike Levinas before him. Deconstruction is not a denial of truth altogether, but opens up to alternatives beyond the narrow confines of conventional distinctions and definitions of truth.

While deconstruction may resemble forms of negative theology, as was also the case with Levinas, it arguably portrays a rather nominalistic suspicion of traditional metaphysics. Obviously, deconstruction cannot be a negative way to a union with something divine beyond language, but must constitute a continuous criticism of our attempts at securing meaning by reducing it to stabilizing first principles. As such, deconstruction can, however, at least be conceived as making possible something akin to *an attitude of apophatic openness* not completely unlike that of traditional negative theology. It should come as no surprise, then, that contemporary theologians and philosophers of religion have taken an interest in deconstruction.

Jean-Luc Nancy (1940–2021), another French philosopher, while initially dismissive of theology and religion altogether, would eventually argue that Christianity has the advantage of containing in itself a tendency towards the deconstruction of metaphysics. Christianity is in and of itself a self-deconstruction, not because God is a hidden God (*deus absconditus*), but because the incarnation of God in Christ in a way undoes theism.[36] Nancy, with reference to Eckhart, explains that faith as such is a faithfulness to the absence of all assurance. This, however, also means that atheism is a Christianity realized rather than something foreign to Christianity. Faith and hope do not need to have any particular object. Similarly, adoration is to be conceived of as an attitude of openness to the infinite possibility beyond language.[37] Rightly

36. Nancy, *Dis-Enclosure*, 35–36.

37. Nancy, *Adoration*, 21–27. See also Newheiser, *Hope in a Secular Age*.

perceived, then, Christian theology leads beyond the metaphysics of traditional religion, while not, for this reason, ending up in the binary alternative of secularism or atheism instead. In this there are parallels between negative theology and deconstruction.

In a similar vein, Mark C. Taylor (1945–) has argued that Derrida's deconstruction is neither simply "theological" nor "atheological," but a/theological in being beyond the binary opposition between the two.[38] In more recent works, John Caputo (1940–) has likewise engaged with deconstruction conceived as a kind of "weak theology." God cannot be defined as "the highest being" since God is not a *thing* at all, but rather an unpredictable event. As event, says Caputo, God adds a level of meaning as well as both provocation and solicitation. As was also argued by, for example, Simone Weil and dialectical theology, as described above, God does not just avail us with meaning and security, but rather makes it impossible for the world to settle solidly or close in on itself.[39] Such theology of the event must, however, be distinguished from classical forms of negative theology and mysticism, argues Caputo, since the latter as "strong theology" only seeks to strengthen a "powerful transcendence" and a strong sense of who is in on the secret and who is not.[40] While this may not be a very fair depiction of classical mystical theology, it does show how deconstruction in theology helps to soften traditional distinctions between faith and secularism, church and world, and so on.

A retrieval of more classical forms of negative theology appears in the French theologian Jean-Luc Marion (1946–), who has argued, in response to the criticism of "onto-theology," that we must conceive of "God without being." As a Roman Catholic theologian, Marion is obviously not arguing that God does not exist, but only that God cannot be reduced to an ontological idea of the "highest being." As also argued by dialectical theology, the "death of God" should be understood as the death of *our metaphysical concepts* of God, which are in fact "idols." The "death of God" is the

38. Taylor, *Erring*, 3–6.
39. Caputo, *The Weakness of God*, 39.
40. Caputo, *The Weakness of God*, 302.

mode of God's *presence* in a secularized world. We may even cross out the word "GxD," says Marion, in order to indicate and recall that God enters into our thought "only in obliging it to criticize itself."[41] Drawing on the Dionysian tradition, Marion importantly adds that God must be thought of as "beyond being" in order to preserve the character of creation as a gift. God is love, but love is nothing in itself, nothing definite or definable, but only something as it gives itself. Revelation is for similar reasons an "icon" rather than an "idol," since it points beyond our metaphysical conceptions of being. If we take things to have their being in and of themselves, they easily become idols, but when we perceive reality as a gift from God, it points beyond itself as an icon. In this way, Marion's approach exemplifies a somewhat less "nihilistic" form of negative theology in a postmodern context, while nevertheless addressing the contemporary need to talk of God beyond traditional metaphysics.

Recently, authors such as Peter Rollins (1973–) have helped popularizing the postmodern critique of certainty, while placing a renewed emphasis on the idea of God as present in absence.[42] This idea characterizes parts of the so-called emerging church movement that popped up around the turn of the millennium as a response to the rise of the "Nones," young people with no religious affiliations, who may nevertheless define themselves as "spiritual" though not "religious." In this context, postmodern negative theology could speak to a non-dogmatic sentiment. There is a certain atheistic spirit in Christianity itself, says Rollins, that not only disbelieves the Pagan gods, but also in some sense disbelieves the God that we believe in. As a/theology, Christian discourse and apologetics cannot use the force of reason, but must be powerless like Christ on the cross. It must protect the ineffable God from being spoken, and instead reveal the love of God in transformed lives. Negative theology thus has some quite practical consequences. As a community of faith, the church is not to seek meaning in the presence of God, but God is to be found in secular society

41. Marion, *God without Being*, 46. See also Marion, *Idol and Distance*.
42. Rollins, *How (Not) to Speak of God*, 5–55.

where God seems to be most absent, in the pub, for example. Only in solidarity with those outside of the church can the church be an icon of God. In this way, the postmodern deconstruction of dichotomies can be fused with a more traditional evangelical concern for mission and evangelism. However, these are now to be conceived not so much as a matter of converting people as of being present in the world where God is present in absence.

It seems, then, that the destruction and deconstruction of metaphysics has not simply led to a wholesale dismissal of traditional theology in the postmodern context. It has also opened up new possibilities for engaging with classical forms of negative theology. Even if negative theology is today rarely engaged in as a "negative way" to God, there does seem to be a renewed interest in the positive, theological aims of traditional negative theology. It may, however, still be necessary to consider on what basis or with what purpose this engagement with negative theology takes place. As should also be clear by now, the reversal of negative theology that occurred from the Reformation period until now may raise the question, is there still more to learn from earlier forms of negative theology?

AFTERWORD

Negative Theology as Radical Orthodoxy?

THE BASIC ARGUMENT IN the three chapters of this book is that negative theology first developed from the convergence of Judaism and Christianity on the one hand with Platonism and Neoplatonism on the other. In this there should be nothing controversial, though the exact details of the story are still disputed. What may seem less obvious is how strains of negative theology can be traced through modern philosophy and theology, even if negative theology has, so to speak, often gone underground in this context. It turns out that negative theology is a complex phenomenon that has evolved throughout history along with the wider theological and philosophical landscape.

The secularization of negative theology arguably raises the question of its future role in theology. Today it may perhaps be asked if negative theology belongs at all in Christian theology, or whether it is not simply a reminiscence of an undue speculative spirit alien to Christianity as such? At any rate, it is not surprising if negative theology may seem at odds with the Christian gospel considered as positive revelation. As argued by, for instance, the later Karl Barth in the twentieth century, God is never "the unknown God," but must always be conceived of as the God who is revealed and known in Jesus Christ.[1] Nevertheless, in spite of the influence of such theological positivism, negative theology continues to pop up in both academic and popular theology and philosophy.

Today, forms of negative theology seem to be enjoying some popularity among those uneasy with too rigid a definition of orthodoxy. For those bruised by conservative religion, negative theology can supply an escape route, a "flight" into the open air. For others, it can serve to open spiritual dimensions beyond the narrow confines of the secular mindset. Whatever the motive for engaging with negative theology, however, there is always the danger that such engagement may become too one-sided and "negativistic," leading to a monotonous rejection of whatever positive perception of the divine or the good others may hold. In its secularized forms, negative theology can even seem to lead to a nihilistic rejection of all positive values. In this form, it risks becoming a more or less unintended ally of the destructive forces of (post)modernity. While older forms of negative theology saw God as the unifying principle beyond all differences, there seems to be little room for unity or participation in the postmodern preoccupation with difference and "the other." To the degree that negative theology can be said to be complicit in this development, this raises the question as to whether negative theology has perhaps come up against a dead end, or whether it may, in fact, still have something to offer.

Recently, theologians associated with the so-called Radical Orthodoxy school have criticized the perceived nihilistic tendencies in postmodern philosophy and theology. As argued not least by John Milbank, the good is not in any way dependent on negation or "nothing." The nominalism of modern philosophy and theology should be countered by a participatory ontology that sees all of reality as in some sense participating in God. They claim that the dialectical thought that can be traced through Hegel to philosophers like Böhme has made negation in the form of evil and destruction necessary to the realization of the good, and it must therefore be rejected as incompatible with Christian theology.

1. Barth, *Prayer*, 25.

Even Jean-Luc Marion's attempt at reviving the Dionysian concept of God as somehow beyond being has been met with suspicion by theologians like David Bentley Hart. We do not need God to be beyond being for creation to be a gift, since God himself represents a perfect trinitarian relationship of infinite love that gives itself in creation.[2]

It has also been noted, however, that Radical Orthodoxy cannot do without a form of negative theology. A theology that seeks to return to the principles of classical Christian philosophy must also be open to the negative theology that was an inherent part of this tradition. William Franke has argued that Radical Orthodoxy can only formulate a legitimate alternative to contemporary nihilism by entering into dialogue with traditions of negative theology. As a positive theology, Radical Orthodoxy, says Franke, is only tenable on the basis of the postmodern rediscovery of negative theology. Radical Orthodoxy should therefore value negative theology, at least as a point of connection to the wider philosophical landscape.[3] Such criticism of Radical Orthodoxy for not appreciating negative theology may seem a bit unfair, however, especially considering John Milbank's and Catherine Pickstock's defense of the classical, analogical approach to theological language (in line with Thomas Aquinas, as described in the above).[4] It is precisely the apophatic element that makes analogy possible. Negative theology is not, for this reason, a particular *kind* of theology, but is rather presupposed in *all* theological language.

It may further be argued, in line with postmodern theology, that the gospel narrative itself contains an apophatic element. Jesus Christ is the incarnate and as such revealed Word of God, but he is also the Word crucified.[5] If the incarnation is the revelation of the Word, the cross is the unsaying or *apophasis* of the self-same Word who must be negated in order to be resurrected in a new, elevated form. The resurrection is love's victorious negation of negation.

2. Hart, *The Beauty of the Infinite*, 237–38.

3. Franke, *A Philosophy of the Unsayable*, 293.

4. Pickstock, *After Writing*, 176–77.

5. Franke, *A Philosophy of the Unsayable*, 68–69.

The gospel narrative thus already implicitly contains the three steps of Dionysian apophaticism. The aim of this process in classical negative theology is not the final negation of all positive meaning and value, but the opening up to an infinite depth of meaning and value that exceeds any finite definition. This is why, even if the incarnation and the cross breaks open every mystery, God's Word nevertheless takes new parabolic and paradoxical forms, as already emphasized by theologians like Clement of Alexandria in the early centuries of Christian thought.

Rather than being at odds, then, with contemporary attempts at retrieving the theological concerns of classical Christian theology as formulated by early theologians, negative theology should be considered *a foundational constituent* of a truly "radical" orthodoxy. It seems clear, however, that not just *any* kind of negative theology will do. There is arguably a need to be skeptical about certain developments in the Neoplatonic concept of God as "beyond being," at least insofar as God becomes indistinguishable from "nothing" or perhaps even from a primordial darkness that makes evil a necessary part of creation. It may be true that postmodern nihilism is, as such, to some degree anticipated in earlier forms of negative theology.[6] This is not, however, a reason for failing to engage with negative theology, but only for listening to those voices that seek to point to a more moderate way that can avoid the extremes of radically negative theologies.

With classical Christian orthodoxy, we may emphasize that negative theology should always be understood against the backdrop of a participatory ontology. This implies a kind of asymmetry between epistemology and ontology: God and the good were not seen as dependent on evil in any way, even if we can only know the good indirectly by negations. It is because God is being itself, in which all beings participate, that God is ineffable and incomprehensible. God is not simply "absent," as claimed by some forms of postmodern negative theology. As the very source of being, God is radically *present*, although in a way that is beyond comprehension.[7]

6. Cunningham, *Genealogy of Nihilism*.

7. As argued by Denys Turner, in classical negative theology God is only

The God that is close to us nevertheless continues to be beyond the grasp of finite human beings. This requires from us an openness to God and reality that defies all attempts at boxing up faith and existence in finite categories. Negative theology has its proper function as a tool to break open language and thought—not because negativity and nothing is the final meaning or truth of everything, or of ourselves as human beings, but because in "the new creation in Christ" (2 Cor 5:17) there are always greater depths of meaning and truth.

Negative theology is not, then, aimed at the negation of meaning and value altogether, but only at avoiding objectifications of the good. While God is not a "something," this also means that God is not somehow instead a "nothing." God is, in other words, not only present in absence, but also in presence. God is not just experienced at the margins, as sometimes claimed, although God is certainly there too. God is also experienced in the church, the liturgy, in preaching and practices of love. With this we are never done. There is always more to say, always more to do. This is why we still need negative theology.

---

absent *if considered as an object of knowledge*, but only because God is so close to us that we cannot observe God as we would observe things like tables and chairs. Turner, *The Darkness of God*, 264.

Suggestions for Further Studies

Carabine, Deirdre. *The Unknown God: Negative Theology in the Platonic Tradition.* 1995. Reprint, Eugene, OR: Wipf & Stock, 2015.

Franke, William. *On What Cannot Be Said, Vol. 1: Classic Formulations.* Notre Dame, IN: University of Notre Dame Press, 2007.

———. *On What Cannot be Said, Vol. 2: Modern and Contemporary Transformations.* Notre Dame, IN: University of Notre Dame Press, 2007.

Gregory of Nyssa. *The Life of Moses.* Translated by Everett Ferguson and Abraham Malherbe. New York: Paulist, 1978.

Nicholas of Cusa. *Selected Spiritual Writings.* New York: Paulist, 1997.

Plotinus. *The Enneads.* London: Penguin, 1991.

Pseudo-Dionysius. *The Complete Works.* New York: Paulist, 1987.

Rollins, Peter. *How (Not) to Speak of God.* London: SPCK, 2006.

Turner, Denys. *The Darkness of God: Negativity in Western Mysticism.* Cambridge: Cambridge University Press, 1999.

Bibliography

Barth, Karl. *The Epistle to the Romans*. Oxford: Oxford University Press, 1933.

——. *Fides quaerens intellectum: Anselm's Proof of the Existence of God in the Context of His Theological Scheme*. Reprint, Eugene, OR: Pickwick, 2009.

——. *Prayer*. Louisville, KY: Westminster John Knox, 2002.

Barth, Karl, and Eduard Thurneysen. *Come Holy Spirit*. Reprint, Eugene, OR: Wipf & Stock, 2009.

Benjamin, Walter. "Theologico-Political Fragment." In *Reflections: Essays, Aphorisms, Autobiographical Writings*, edited by Peter Demetz, 312–13. New York: Harcourt Brace Jovanovich, 1978.

Berdyaev, Nicolai. *The Divine and the Human*. Translated by R. M. French. San Rafael, CA: Semantron, 2009.

——. "Studies Concerning Jacob Boehme." *Etude II. Journal Put'* 21 (1930) 47–79.

Blumenberg, Hans. *The Legitimacy of the Modern Age*. Cambridge: MIT Press, 1985.

Böhme, Jacob. *Sämmtliche Werke*. Leipzig: Barth, 1832–60.

Brewer, Talbot. *The Retrieval of Ethics*. Oxford: Oxford University Press, 2009.

Bulhof, Ilse N., and Laurens ten Kate. *Flight of the Gods: Philosophical Perspectives on Negative Theology*. Kampen: Kok Agora, 2000.

Caputo, John. *The Weakness of God: A Theology of the Event*. Bloomington, IN: Indiana University Press, 2006.

Carabine, Deirdre. *The Unknown God: Negative Theology in the Platonic Tradition*. 1991. Reprint, Eugene, OR: Wipf & Stock, 2015.

Conley, John J. *The Other Pascals: The Philosophy of Jacqueline Pascal, Gilberte Pascal Périer, and Marguerite Périer*. Notre Dame, IN: University of Notre Dame Press, 2019.

Cunningham, Conor. *Genealogy of Nihilism*. London: Routledge, 2002.

Daniélou, Jean. *From Glory to Glory: Texts from Gregory of Nyssa's Mystical Writings*. New York: Scribner, 1961.

Denck, Hans. *Religiöse Schriften, vol. 2*. Gütersloh: Mohn, 1960.

Derrida, Jacques. "Différance." In *Margins of Philosophy*, 1–28. Translated by Alan Bass. Chicago: University of Chicago Press, 1982.

Bibliography

———. "How to Avoid Speaking: Denials." In *Derrida and Negative Theology*, edited by Harold Coward et al., 73–142. Albany, NY: State University of New York Press, 1992.

Eckhart, Meister. *Selections from His Essential Writings*. New York: Harper One, 1957.

Fagenblat, Michael. Ed. *Negative Theology as Jewish Modernity*. Bloomington, IN: Indiana University Press, 2017.

Finlayson, Gordon. "Notes on Negative Theology and Adorno's Negative Dialectics." JHIBlog. 2021. https://jhiblog.org/2021/04/29/notes-on-negative-theology-and-adornos-negative-dialectics/.

Franke, William. *Apophatic Paths from Europe to China: Regions without Borders*. New York: SUNY Press, 2018.

———. *On the Universality of What Is Not: The Apophatic Turn in Critical Thinking*. Notre Dame, IN: University of Notre Dame Press, 2020.

———. *On What Cannot be Said, Vol. 1: Classic Formulations*. Notre Dame, IN: University of Notre Dame Press, 2007.

———. *On What Cannot be Said, Vol. 2: Modern and Contemporary Transformations*. Notre Dame, IN: University of Notre Dame Press, 2007.

———. *A Philosophy of the Unsayable*. Notre Dame, IN: University of Notre Dame Press, 2014.

Guthrie, W. C. K. *A History of Greek Philosophy, Vol. 5*. Cambridge: Cambridge University Press, 1978.

Hägg, Henny F. *Clement of Alexandria and the Beginnings of Christian Apophaticism*. Oxford: Oxford University Press, 2006.

Hart, David Bentley. *The Beauty of the Infinite*. Eugene, OR: Eerdmans, 2003.

———. *The Experience of God: Being, Consciousness, Bliss*. New Haven, CT: Yale University Press, 2013.

———. *The Hidden and the Manifest: Essays in Theology and Metaphysics*. Grand Rapids: Eerdmans, 2017.

Hegel, G. W. F. *Phenomenology of Spirit*. Translated by A. V. Miller. Oxford: Oxford University Press, 1977.

Horstmann, Johannes. "Kristendom og existens I" *Tidehverv* 36 (1962) 65–69.

———. "Kristendom og existens II" *Tidehverv* 36 (1962) 79–88.

Jugrin, Daniel. "The One Beyond Silence: The Apophatic Henology of Proclus." *Philosophia* 1 (2019) 63–87.

Jüngel, Eberhard. *God as the Mystery of the World: On the Foundation of the Theology of the Crucified One in the Dispute between Theism and Atheism*. London: Bloomsbury, 2014.

Karamanolis, George. *The Philosophy of Early Christianity*. Abingdon, UK: Routledge, 2021.

Kierkegaard, Søren. *Concluding Unscientific Postscript to Philosophical Fragments*. Kierkegaard's Writings. Princeton: Princeton University Press, 2013.

———. *Fear and Trembling*. Kierkegaard's Writings. Princeton: Princeton University Press, 2013.

Bibliography

——. *Journals NB26-NB30*. Søren Kierkegaard's Journals and Notebooks. Princeton: Princeton University Press, 2017.

Kline, Peter. *Passion for Nothing: Kierkegaard's Apophatic Theology*. Minneapolis: Fortress, 2017.

Knepper, Timothy D., et al. *Ineffability: An Exercise in Comparative Philosophy of Religion*. Cham, Switzerland: Springer, 2017.

Law, David R. *Kierkegaard as Negative Theologian*. Oxford: Oxford University Press, 1993.

Levinas, Emmanuel. *Totality and Infinity: An Essay on Exteriority*. London: Kluwer Academic, 1969.

——. "Meaning and Sense." In *Collected Philosophical Papers*, 75–107. Dordrecht: Springer, 1987.

Luther, Martin. *D. Martin Luthers Werke*. Weimar: H. Böhlaus Nachfolger, 1883–2009.

——. *On the Bondage of the Will. D. Martin Luthers Werke*, vol 18. Weimar: H. Böhlaus Nachfolger, 1883–2009.

——. *Tischreden, Vol. 6*. Weimar: H. Böhlau, 1912–21.

Marion, Jean-Luc. *God without Being: Hors-Texte, Second Edition*. Chicago: University of Chicago Press, 1991.

——. *The Idol and Distance: Five Studies*. New York: Fordham University Press, 2001.

——. "Is the Ontological Argument Ontological?" In *Flight of the Gods*, edited by Ilse N. Bulhof and Laurens ten Kate, 78–99. Kampen: Kok Agora, 2000.

Mjaaland, Marius Timman. *The Hidden God*. Bloomington, IN: Indiana University Press, 2016.

Moltmann, Jürgen. *The Crucified God*. Minneapolis: Fortress, 2015.

Moran, Dermot. *The Philosophy of John Scotus Eriugena: A Study of Idealism in the Middle Ages*. Cambridge: Cambridge University Press, 1989.

Mortley, Raoul. *From Word to Silence, Vol. 2: The Way of Negation, Christian and Greek*. Bonn: Hanstein, 1986.

Moss, Gregory S. "The Problem of Evil in the Speculative Mysticism of Meister Eckhart." In *The Problem of Evil: New Philosophical Directions*, edited by Benjamin W. McCraw and Robert Arp, 45–50. Lanham, MD: Lexington, 2016.

Nancy, Jean-Luc. *Adoration: The Deconstruction of Christianity II*. New York: Fordham University Press, 2013.

——. *Dis-Enclosure: The Deconstruction of Christianity*. New York: Fordham University Press, 2008.

Newbigin, Lesslie. *The Gospel in a Pluralist Society*. Grand Rapids: Eerdmans, 1989.

Newheiser, David. *Hope in a Secular Age: Deconstruction, Negative Theology and the Future of Faith*. Cambridge: Cambridge University Press, 2020.

Pickstock, Catherine. *After Writing: On the Liturgical Consummation of Philosophy*. Oxford: Blackwell, 1998.

Bibliography

Radde-Gallwitz, Andrew. *Basil of Caesarea, Gregory of Nyssa, and the Transformation of Divine Simplicity.* Oxford: Oxford University Press, 2009.

Rollins, Peter. *How (Not) to Speak of God.* London: SPCK, 2006.

Rosenzweig, Franz. *The Star of Redemption.* Boston: Beacon, 1972.

Schelling, F. W. J. *The Ages of the World.* Ann Arbor, MI: The University of Michigan Press, 1997.

———. *Philosophical Investigations into the Essence of Human Freedom.* Albany, NY: State University of New York Press, 2006.

Sokolowski, Robert. *The God of Faith and Reason: Foundations of Christian Theology.* Washington, DC: Catholic University of America, 1995.

Steenbuch, Johannes Aakjær. "A Christian Anarchist? Gregory of Nyssa's Criticism of Political Power." *Political Theology* 17 (2016) 573–88.

Stępień, Tomasz, and Karolina Kochańczyk-Bonińska. *Unknown God, Known in His Activities: Incomprehensibility of God during the Trinitarian Controversy of the 4th Century.* Frankfurt am Main: Peter Lang, 2018.

Taylor, Mark C. *Erring: A Postmodern A/theology.* Chicago: University of Chicago Press, 1987.

Turner, Denys. "Apophaticism, Idolatry and the Claims of Reason." In *Silence and the Word*, edited by Oliver Davies and Denys Turner, 11–34. Cambridge: Cambridge University Press, 2002.

———. *The Darkness of God: Negativity in Western Mysticism.* Cambridge: Cambridge University Press, 1999.

Weil, Simone. *Gravity and Grace.* Translated by Emma Crawford. London: Routledge and Kegan Paul, 1963.

Wolfson, Harry A. "Albinus and Plotinus on Divine Attributes." *Harvard Theological Review* 45 (1952) 115–30.

Zimmermann, Nigel. *Levinas and Theology.* London: Bloomsbury T. & T. Clark, 2013.